Getting Old
Sucks!

by *Ernie del Santo*

Illustrated by Tom Cain

Ernie del Santo

"Getting Old Sucks!"

Burbank Publishing
212 S. Reese Pl.
Burbank, California 91506

Burbankpublishing@gmail.com

ISBN 9780984195039

Illustrations and Cover by Thomas Cain

So I was walking past a 7-11 the other day, and this 9-year old Tubbo was standing outside eating a cookie as big as his head, and was giving his dog some of it.
His mother comes out of the store with a Slurpee the size of the Water Tower and a bag of gummy worms. She tells the kid, "Don't give that to the dog; it's not good for him!"

I wanted to tell her, "For chrissakes, lady, forget the dog. Why don't you worry about the shit you're feeding your kid?"

So I did.

That didn't go well.

Ernie del Santo

This book is dedicated to the most patient and loving woman God ever put on this Earth. When people say to me "I can't believe SHE married YOU!" I just shrug my shoulders and admit I have no idea how it happened. But it did, and I'm a damn lot better man for it. Marie is the best, and I will love her 'til I die. Which may come sooner than I'd like.

Ernie del Santo

*"Under certain circumstances, profanity
provides a relief denied even to prayer"*

\- Mark Twain -

Contents

Ernie del Santo

"I don't fear too many things. I grew up in Chicago. With nuns."

LET'S GET THIS THING STARTED

The other day two of my grandkids were in the kitchen while I was making 'em breakfast. Both sitting two feet from each other, but on their cell phones the whole time. After they eat, they give me their plates and as they walk out (you didn't think they were gonna help, did you?) Sam starts laughing and says, *"Grandpa's phone hangs on the wall with a noodle-cord on it."* "Cro-Magnon man!" *"We should get a Sharpie and draw an app on it. Ha ha!"*

I picked up the dog's tennis ball, aimed that slimy sucker right at the back of his head and threw my best fastball. Missed him by a foot and a half. Getting old sucks.

Suddenly I'm staring into the mirror and an old fart is staring back. There's a brown spot on my forehead up by my hairline that wasn't there before. A hair out of a mole; worse yet, out of my frickin' ear? I flex, but I can't see the muscles in my arms like I used to. Maybe it's these glasses.

Sometimes I look in that mirror and I still see traces of that young strong del Santo stud that I was, and can still muster up once in a blue moon. But nobody ever got into the ring with Father Time and came out a winner. So ok,

Ernie del Santo

I'm old. But I've been married to the same woman for over 40 years and we have three kids and five grandkids. At least I got something to show for it.

Why the book? Guys in the neighborhood or in the bowling alley always want to tell me stories about their internal ailments, or their backaches or how their new diet isn't keeping their weight down enough so their big ass will fit in the seat on Southworst Airlines and not spill over onto the unfortunate clown in the middle seat.

And when they talk, they usually end up with "You know what I mean, Ernie?" And I usually try to end their blathering with *"Do I know? Are you kidding me? I could write a frickin' book."*

So I am.

But this isn't a 'oh woe is me' bitch book; it's not all about bad backs, laxatives, loss of stamina at the wrong times, peeing in the middle of the night, or your ball-sack hanging lower than it used to. I might mention those things 'cause they're all true, but so is this: 'If you don't have a bad back by this age, you weren't doing nothing.'

And getting old may suck, but I prefer it to getting dead. I passed up Errol Flynn and Bogart's age a long time ago. They had a lot of fun in their lives but they hit the dirt early. Me and my friends had some high-flying days too in our youth; I got the scars to prove it. But now we're paying for it. So be it.

I try to follow Ben Franklin's advice and keep my vices 'in moderation'. People say things like "hey, you're looking good" or "you're pretty strong", and that's nice. But before the compliment can cause a stirring in my loins, they add *"for your age"* and that pisses me off. Screw them; I'd rather be old and playing in the 'senior league' than six feet under.

I'll tell you a quick story since you're good enough to still be reading this even though the book hasn't really started yet. A story about memory and tattoos.

The Scars To Prove It   One night about 45 years ago I go out with some of my loudmouth buddies to a bar called *The Wild Hare* on the South Side. Just so happens the guy from a gin company is there and all gin drinks are a quarter apiece. And we got our money's worth.

Well, my friend Butch gets obnoxious with a couple of girls who knew one of the bartenders, and the bouncers escort him out. But bouncers back then were generally frat-house asshats, so they also pop him one on the side of the head for good measure. I didn't see it, just saw the bloody result, but I figured he deserved it so I grabbed him and walked him away from 'em.

Then one of the bigger bouncers chases after us and keeps harassing him as we walk to my car. I can only keep

Butch quiet for just so long; finally Butch tells the guy "blow me, asshole" and turns away.

But the guy, who's bigger than both of us, is gonna cold-cock Butch so I push his arm and tell him "don't do it." The Bouncer just wants to hit somebody so he turns on me and throws a haymaker toward my face.

Now, I may not have been the best boxer the CYO ever saw, but even on 'twenty-five cents for a gin and tonic night' I can block your punch if you swing from your hip.

So I block his haymaker and the natural thing to do at that point is to throw the right. So I hit him with a straight right to the jaw and down he went. Bam.

Bad move. His bouncer friends were right behind me. Three of 'em. And me half in the bag. Did I mention drinks were a quarter apiece? I got a few shots in, but basically got pummeled a bit before someone yelled that the cops were coming. Rough night.

So now, when kids ask me if I have any tattoos, I say "*nope; I have scars*". Same thing, they both tell a story. And I show 'em the Wild Hare scar next to my left eye.

I remember that night like it was last week. Last week? That I don't remember so much. So it goes. Wish I could still throw a straight right like that, though. Damn I was good, and the older I get, the better I was.

Ok, get your reading glasses on and let's get started. There may be times when I go out of order, and times when I repeat myself. Comes with the territory. The title ain't "Getting Old is Lovely." Let's go.

Ernie del Santo

THE GOOD, THE BAD, AND
THE ERNIE

I was coming out of the shower the other day and suddenly my ankle gave out. Just collapsed on me. I started to fall, recovered, then braced myself against the wall, and as I'm trying to twist it around and get some feeling back in it, my wife Marie yells out *"What happened?"* I tell her it's just my ankle, no big deal; it's fine.

She then 'inquires,' *"What did you do to it?"*

"What did I DO? Well, let's see, it must've been that marathon I was running in Boston yesterday. After 20 miles I was on Heartbreak Hill and this midget runs up next to me and starts to pass me. He's really moving, so I decide to push it because I'll be damned if I'm losing a foot-race to a 4-foot --- HOW DO I KNOW?! I didn't DO anything to it! It just happened."

I can't remember a time when something didn't hurt; when I didn't feel like I had an injury. My shoulders, my hip, … I have to wear a knee brace when I do roadwork ('jogging'). Not that I'm not used to it—I was an athlete,

I'm used to being injured. I played ball for 40 years and I used to box in college, so I've torn ligaments and muscles before.

But for chrissakes, now I'm just on a bowling team; not exactly a contact sport.

And when I was young and I got injured, I knew HOW I got injured. I got hit, I tripped in a hole while I was running, or I tried to put the old fridge in the back of the pickup by myself and it slipped onto my foot. I knew how I got hurt. Now the injuries… just happen.

God I miss being young and strong. And I miss my former height. When I was 18 and going off to college I was a shade over 5'10 ½ ". After my junior year I was 6-foot. Now I'm back to around 5'10 ½ ". I guess drinking and screwing around makes you tall.

Now, I creak. Half the joints in my frickin' body---loud cracks that you can hear from the next room. I guess I can give up the idea of ever being a private eye because I couldn't sneak up on anybody. Every morning the joints in my back, knees and ankles sounds like the creaky doors in a Vincent Price movie.

But I knew these days were coming. I saw it all the time when I was a kid delivering papers … old men a little hunched over walking around, always looking like they're either constipated or mad at something.

Leon Trotsky once said, *"Old age is the most unexpected of things that can happen to a man."* That's bullshit. We may have denied it, and pretended that we'd be ten-foot tall and bulletproof all our life, but we knew better. We knew it was coming.

When I was young I spent a couple of my high school summers working on a farm with a 70-year old man named Barney. When it was time to throw bales of hay, Barney would walk up to 'em with me, look at them for a few seconds, rub his face, then tell me "give 'em two flakes each and throw the rest of the bales up there."

I could tell he wanted to throw 'em up there himself, but he couldn't. One day he just said to me, *"There'll be a time when you can't do this either. And you're gonna miss being strong."* You're gonna miss being strong.

It's here and I'm him. I've gone from being the guy you called when you needed something heavy moved, to *"Here, Dad, let me help you with that."* And it sucks.

Selective Memory   Most of my family are smartasses, and because they're family they think they can say anything they want to your face and get away with it … just because they're family.

And one of the things they tell me is that my memory is shot. My memory is not shot. It's more selective. Sometimes I don't remember where I put my keys, but so what? I got other things on my mind. I remember how to change an electrical plug in the wall and which circuit runs the bathroom fan, but do I remember the name of my wife's cousin in Indiana? No, 'cause she's a pain in the ass.

Do I remember my dad letting me skip school one day so we could go to Comiskey on his day off? Yeah. I do. We got seats down the third base line, not too far up from the dugout and Early Wynn pitched a gem. In the fifth inning, Sherm Lollar---the catcher---he hit a home run so far I swear they're still looking for it. I remember that.

My brain still works. It's just selective. And so is my attention. I don't pretend that I can do six things at a time. I don't multi-task; I focus.

But I do have some friends, and some friends of friends, that have Alzheimer's or some other degenerative brain disease, and it's tragic to watch. I genuinely hope there's a reward in the next life for all the shit they're going through now.

Thin Skin   In every sense of the word. It used to be that I'd come home with a gash in my hand or my arm and wonder 'when the hell did that happen?' I'd hit something hard or sharp and wouldn't even feel it.

Now I just walk past the edge of the end table and it reaches up and attacks my forearm and the next thing you know I'm bleeding like Chuck Wepner.

Same thing when I'm wrestling with my dog, Rocky Balboa. He's half Pointer, half Lab and all dog. And if his claw barely scrapes across my wrist I'm dripping.

And the other thin skin…I don't suffer fools as easily as I used to. Don't get me wrong, I'm not the old fart who yells at everybody and thinks he's entitled to say and do whatever he wants because he's old. The world doesn't owe us anything just because we've been here longer. But there're a lot of idiots out there, and the numbers of 'em seem to be growing exponentially. Assholism must be the biggest religion in the world, 'cause there's sure a lot of zealots.

You know the old saying **"*People in pain are a pain in the ass*"**? Maybe it's not an old saying; I might have made it up. But anyway, I gotta watch out or I'll be the pain in the ass myself 'cause like I said ---lots of things hurt, on the outside and on the inside. Thank God for ibuprofen and back braces.

[Quick note on back braces: I have a couple of 'em, and they have saved me many times. I cinch that thing up and I can stand up straight and walk in the worst of times. Which makes me hope that the guy who invented Velcro made a truckload of money. He deserved it.]

This thin skin can be … inconvenient, shall we say, or even dangerous. Sometimes I'm just making a point, and it only SOUNDS like I'm a complaining old fart.

Case in point: Marie walks to the front door and opens it, forgets her purse and walks back to the bedroom. Front door wide open and it's 46 degrees out. If I say anything, I'm a complainer. If I don't, the damn furnace kicks on and starts the Con Ed robbery.

I'm damned if I don't just get up and go close the door. So I do … the first five times. Then I get a little annoyed, shall we say, and raise my voice a tiny bit. And now I'm a pain in the ass – 'why don't I just relax?' So I relax. And hope she can do the same tonight, with the crinkly electric bill stuffed inside her pillowcase.

Iron and Steel   Thinking about that baseball game with my dad makes me wish he'd made it to old age. He was a hard working guy, started in the foundry right after 8th grade. When someone asked him if he went to high school he said, 'I went by it.'

We didn't have the money other kids had, but he tried hard for us and showed us how to make money delivering papers, sweeping out stores and stacking shelves; stuff like that. We had all the advantages of being poor and didn't think a thing about it.

But he smoked, and ate what men ate back then. He died before he ever met my wife Marie. He would have liked Marie; they would have had a lot of laughs together.

One thing both my parents wanted for me and my brothers was a good education, and we went to college.

Ernie del Santo

To pay for it I worked summers in the steel mill along Lake Michigan, on the furnaces in the coke plant. I worked with a lot of good people in that mill, guys who were going to be there for a long time working on the furnace lids, the hot car, on the wharf.

I started out shoveling coke and coal back on to conveyor belts that sent it over to the steel side. Then I was 'promoted' over to the furnaces and issued a small jackhammer. My job was to hook up the push car, clean the huge furnace doors, wait for it to push the red-hot coke into the hot car, get the door closed and then move on to the next one.

Almost Cooked   The furnaces were two stories high, so I could never see the hot car; I could only see the big hunk of steel push into the furnace and then come back. When it did, it dropped some red-hot coal on the deck, and I would shovel it up and throw it back in to the furnace before we closed the door.

One time the hot car took a long time, so I hooked it up and went about my cleaning. I didn't hear the whistle indicating it was ready, and the man in the push car didn't see me standing right in front of the furnace. So he started the pusher arm …. right toward me.

You know how sometimes you can just feel a presence behind you? I did, and so I turned, just in time to see the big 3,000-pound hunk of steel about to push my body into the red-hot furnace. It touched the bill on my hardhat; one more second and I'm toast --- literally.

I quickly dropped to the deck and it went over me into the furnace. Then I rolled away just as several pounds of hot coke fell right where I had been lying. Would have landed squarely on my back, killing me within seconds.

All I could hear was my heart beating, and the loud laughter from the man in the push car. *"Hahaha ... sumbitch, I ain't never seen anybody move so fast. Hahaha."* Glad I could provide some comedy on a hot and sweaty day. I was fast back then. Not so much anymore.

There was an old black man (what?) named Earl that had been in that steel mill for 30 years, and he and I used to sit on a couple of two-by-sixes stretched over some buckets in between the furnaces. We had some memorable talks on our breaks. He'd light up a Kool and start telling stories about growing up in Detroit, hitchhiking across the country, things he'd learned and the crap he took all along the way.

He had a great sense of humor, a great laugh. Proud of his kids. It was as much of an education as I got at ISU, just a different subject. Life.

Me and Harry Chapin After I graduated (and after some time that Uncle Sam borrowed) Marie and I got married and I took a job with Ford Motor. Wore a suit

and tie, drove a company car, had it made. Got promoted
to a travel district which meant more money, but I was out
of town a lot.

So one week I was in Toledo and trying to wrap up the
meetings and seminars early so I could get back to my
brother Vinnie's birthday party in Chicago. Marie was
pregnant with Beth, and she could've used my help.

I called my boss and said I wanted to leave on Thursday;
that nothing productive or profitable was going to happen
on Friday.   My boss says no. I tell him it's important to
make it home; my family needs me there.   *"Is your family
paying you?! Because we are, and your job this week is
in Toledo. Are we clear?"*   What a jackass.

I stay through Friday, wasting my time glad-handing and
buying already-drunk salesmen more drinks and lunches.
And as I'm driving back through Indiana, Harry Chapin's
new song 'Cats In The Cradle' comes on the radio. I
listened to every word: *"...but there were planes to catch
and bills to pay; he learned to walk while I was away."*
Was the best damn songwriting I ever heard, and hit me
like a shovel to the side of the head.

I thought about it the whole way home. *"Can you teach
me to throw? I said 'not today, I got a lot to do'.."* Was I
just chasing money--- money that I'd never had in my
whole life until now--- and missing some of the things
Harry was singing about? I spent a lot of nights studying
my ass off so I could get good grades and get a good job.

And now I've got a good-paying job. Do I want to piss that away?

Luck was in my corner. A few days later I was holding my son on my lap watching a Bulls game when the phone rings. Marie tells me it's the manager of the post office. The post office?

About 5 years earlier I wasn't sure the steel mill would be hiring, so I applied for a summer job at the post office. Took the federal test, turned in the application, but I never heard back from 'em and I got my old job on the furnace. So I forgot all about it. Now, here they are calling. They finally had a job opening...over 5 years later.

Didn't pay as much money as Ford and no company car, but it came with a pension and I'd be home every night. And since I now had a degree, they could put me on a manager track. So, am I a businessman or a family man?

I grabbed that job with both hands and never looked back. I coached all of my boys' baseball games and sat through every single one of my daughter's recitals.

Harry Chapin helped change my life, and I was one sad sonuvabitch when he got in that car accident. Harry never got to get old, and that really sucks.

I stayed at the post office the rest of my working days; the last fifteen I was the manager. And believe me, they tested my managerial skills.

Ernie del Santo

If you've ever been to a post office around here you know that we have people that are good, capable, solid folks; and some that are as dumb as a hundred chickens. I figured my job was not to make them great, but to make them better.

I tried to be a fair boss, good to the workers but not taking any shit either. And if they had a family function that was really important to them, we found a way. You treat the employees right and you don't have to worry about the customers.

They appreciated it and threw me a big party at the end. That made me feel good, 'cause in previous years we had a couple of real pricks for bosses.

Saw a couple of boys with their skateboards out in front of the water department, and they had the baggy pants that hang off their ass and the underwear sticking out the top. I looked at their pants with my usual cheery disposition, and they challenged me... "What's the matter old man, never seen shorts before?" *I said,* "Yeah, sure, we had those when I was your age. All the little girls wore them. Called 'em 'culottes'."

They didn't see the humor.

Ernie del Santo

DAMN KIDS

Like I said, I love my kids and would do anything for 'em, but damn they age the hell out of you. Happens a little bit at a time, like a Chinese water torture. Half of the gray hairs on my head are from watching one of my sons almost fall out of a tree, or twist his ankle sliding into third, or watching my teenage daughter get into a car with some salivating prick and ride off into the night.

But I miss 'em being around. And I'm losing my knowledge of 'em too. I didn't mind losing my grip; my influence on them dropped off the cliff a long time ago, and I'm fine with that. They're good adults now. But, well, here...

Tools Not too long ago it was my oldest son Tony's birthday and they were over at our place. Tony works around his house a lot so I decided to give a real gift; not just some lame gift card. I'll shop for him like some 'Father Knows Best' dad would do. I'll get him some tools.

So I go to Sears and buy him some nice craftsman tools in a leather pouch. When I give them to him he's really appreciative; I did a good job, a real present.   At the end of his party they're all leaving and after I close the door I go over and look out the window. What do I see?

My older son hands his present to my younger son and says, "Here, I don't need these; I've got every tool I need. You want 'em?"

So Michael, the artist who doesn't know a crescent wrench from a crescent moon, he gets the tools.

As I watch them all get into their cars I realize I don't know them as well as I thought; as well as I want to. I thought I did, but they've been gone a long time. Father doesn't know best anymore.

Half the time I look out the window they're still 8 and 6 and 4 years old and they still live here, still play in the yard. I miss being a full-time dad. I like being with them and I'm still their dad and I always will be…but I miss being a full-time dad. It used to be that there was never any quiet in our house; now there's too much.

Don't get me wrong; raising these three wasn't a picnic without ants. And I probably did better with the boys than I did with our daughter Beth. Marie did that job very well and Beth turned out to be a beautiful woman, inside and out, just like her mother.

"Come ti vidi m'innamorai, e tu sorridi perché lo sai."

Infatuation. I'll tell you one thing I did for Beth that I'm kinda proud of ... there weren't many times I was the ideal dad for her, so indulge me, ok? One night she comes home from a date and Marie was already asleep.

Beth is upset because she thinks this guy is going to ask her to be engaged and she doesn't feel like she's ready; that it's too early in the relationship.

Beth probably thinks I'm going to say something like *'dump this horny worthless sonovabitch and move on'* but I don't. I want to, but I don't.

Instead we sit down at the kitchen table with a glass of Amaretto. After listening to her story I add my two cents.

I tell her that there's a reason why "in love" is two words and "infatuation" is only one. There's a space between the words 'in love', and there needs to be a space in that emotion. Some time. There's no space in the word infatuation; it's instant. But 'in love' is deeper, and requires time, space.

Don't marry the first schmoe you become infatuated with; that's not 'in love'. Not yet. Might turn out that way, but give it some space. If he's the one, he'll wait. If he doesn't want to wait, get rid of the bum. Life's too short.

She smiled a sad smile, clinked her glass with mine and said *"Salùte"*, just like she used to do with her milk glass years ago. I told her I love her and went to bed.

A month later they were kaput. Horny bastard couldn't wait out the time, so good riddance. Beth had some heartbreak along the way, but four years later said 'yes' to the right guy and I walked her down the aisle. One of the proudest days of my life. They are still happily married and –no brag, just fact – partly thanks to me.

My reward for that great advice? Being kept on my toes by their daughter Maggie Marie. The granddaughter who considers it her job to let me know when I fall asleep in my chair with my mouth open, and to examine my face and point out every oddity that is evidence of my expired youth.

You Think It's Funny But It's Snot   She informs me, a little too often, when I have a nose-hair extending so much as one millimeter beyond the tip of my nostril.

"It's growing out of all the snot up there; it's probably got like a million-zillion germs on that one hair. Gross, Grandpa!"

Once she was watching me clip them with some fingernail clippers and she shrieked, causing me to cut my nostril and look like Jack Nicholson in Chinatown. *"Agghh! I am never using those clippers again, now they have germy blood all over them! Where's the Purell?!"*

I actually enjoyed watching her go crazy, but just try to blow your nose and not re-open that quarter-inch canal running through it. That doesn't blow; it sucks.

Having grandkids around the house isn't the same as having kids. A little harder because I'm older, but sometimes it's better because I can have a lot more fun and screw with their heads --- then send 'em home. First time around I had to try to be the responsible parent.

I probably was more responsible and patient with the first two, Tony and Beth. By the time Michael came around, I was usually 'cut to the chase'.

Stretch Socks   One time when Michael was about 15 or 16 it was Sunday and I was doing the laundry (yeah, real men do laundry, fuck off) and I see one of his athletic socks, and it's got stains on it. Familiar stains.

I calmly ask him "what the hell is this?" He goes in to a long tale about analgesic on his ankle, dirt in the infield, him sliding in to break up the double play blah blah blah. I listen to this shit for a while just to see if he's a good storyteller.

Finally I say to him: *"Hold it. Listen, if you're gonna jack off in your sock, don't put it in the laundry where your mother can find it. You think she doesn't know what dried cum looks like? How do you think you got here? Show your mother some respect and use your hands for something else, like washing this out in the basin."*

We never had to have that talk again, and in spite of me he turned out ok. A creative type; writer, artist, thinker. He works for a marketing firm, but he comes and goes as he pleases. Writes and draws some great stuff for them that has landed in a lot of magazines and on tv.

Race   About 3 years ago Michael was dating, and then got engaged to a girl named Lena who was three-quarter Bahamian. Beautiful, sharp girl who, at first …maybe because I'm an old profane crusty prick … was worried that I wouldn't be able to accept a girl into the family that was darker-skinned than everybody else.

One night after they got engaged, she found me and Rocky sitting out on the front porch, and she sat down and brought up the whole race issue. I was kind of surprised at the questions. *"You think I might not want you for my son just because you're half black? What I want for that knucklehead is a good woman, period. And you are. I'm just happy you wanted him. You're the best thing that could happen to him."*

As far as race is concerned, I told her the only race I cared about was the one when Michael was 12.

At the end of his baseball practices I used to tell his team if any of them ever beat me to the centerfield pole and back to home plate, I'd buy them all breakfast at IHop. And for years I never lost. But finally when he was 12, on the run back to home plate late in the season, two kids beat me. And I knew I'd never win that sprint again.

That's the only race I care about. The rest is all crap. Nobody picks their parents.

Michael and Lena are married now, and Lena and I get along great. She thinks I'm funny. Marie tells her "don't encourage him" but she does. I like her. I wouldn't have been happier if he'd married Gabriela Sabatini. That's the truth.

But that race with the baseball team still pisses me off; I thought for sure I could out-run those kids at least until they were 13. Getting old sucks, and it costs money.

Buy What You Like   Speaking of money …. ever since the kids were little I've had them save some of their money for the future; birthday money, money they made around the block mowing yards or shoveling snow, babysitting, cleaning out gutters—-that kind of thing.

But instead of a bank, I had them invest it. I have a friend who's a broker and he set them up with stock accounts, where they could buy what they liked. I mean that literally---what they liked. I gave them some advice, but not that much.

Tony liked Fritos so he bought stock in that (Pepsi). He reasoned that every time he ate a bag he was helping himself. Beth made some money babysitting and knew that Barbie was a big deal, so her first stock was Mattel.

They learned business by osmosis and didn't realize it because they were having fun with it. They bought Hershey, Kellogg's; Kraft because they loved macaroni.

When Tony was little he used to like to watch construction backhoes work, so his second stock was John Deere.

And Michael, who loved to see the big buildings downtown, invested in John Hancock. We used to drive past The Hancock by Lake Michigan and he'd look up and ask, *"Dad, do you think I have enough to own one of those windows yet?"* "Two windows, buddy. Those two way up there. Those are yours."

When they turned 18 they had some money, and knew a little bit about dividends and stock splits.

Dangerous Liaisons   Last thing on 'kids'---some advice I gave to Tony and Michael some years ago: not all women are like your mother. If you go out to a party and some girl that you just met gets a little drunk, and agrees to go home with you and 'show you a few things', you didn't just get lucky. You got unlucky.

That's not the kind of girl you want. *"Do you think your sister would ever go home with some schmoe that she just met in a club? And if you say 'yes' first I'm gonna thump you, then I'm gonna go over and thump her one."* (She takes off her headphones and says 'what?!' I think she got that expression from me).

The point is, when you hear *'she's not easy, she's a cinch'* stay away. Let your friends tell the doctor 'it stings when I pee', not you. Stick with the ones you know.

Ernie del Santo

THINGS THAT PISS ME OFF

You probably think by now: 'a charming guy like you never gets pissed off, right?' Well, you know the old saying *"Illegitimus non carborundum est"*? It's *"Don't let the bastards grind you down."*   But sometimes … they do.

We all have stuff that pisses us off, and most of those things have pissed us off all of our lives … like guys that are always late, or clowns who cut you off in traffic with no warning, then put their brakes on. Or the ones who get near the intersection when the light is green but put on their brakes anyway because *"I don't know, it might turn red…"*

Yeah, sometime in the near future it will turn red, but right now it's GREEN so get the hell going! Wonder why some drivers give you the finger? That's why. You're welcome. (I got a story about traffic lights that I'll tell you later).

The little things that piss us off----ladies that wait until their groceries are completely bagged before they pull out their coupons, and then start searching in a 10-gallon purse for their credit card---I'm not talking about that stuff. There are asshats everywhere and it's been that way our whole life.

Scammers I'm talking about the stuff that happens to you when you get old. Like scammers. They target old folks because they're easy marks. One day I'd like to walk past one of 'em when they're pretending to be the IRS or some other government agency, trying to scam someone out of their retirement money.

On second thought, maybe not. I might go Tony Soprano on 'em and end up in jail. (But the IRS isn't gonna call you! And some prick that calls and says your computer needs immediate attention is lying!)

Here's one that for the life of me I don't know how people still fall for it: my friend Mike ran in to an older neighbor of his at the bank; she was panicked because her grandson was in a jail in Mexico and needed money to get out. The 'grandson' just called her and asked her to send 1800 bucks to this 'cop' and he'd release him from the jail.

"You just talked to him?" "*Yes.*" "You're sure it was him?" "*Yes. Well, he sounded different because his nose was broken; they broke his nose when they arrested him.*

Ernie del Santo

And they took his phone. I can't call him. He's in trouble!"

Mike takes her cell phone, asks his name, looks up his number in her phone book and calls it. The grandson answers. *"Hey, is this Brian? This is your grandmother's neighbor Mike; she and I are at the bank. How you doing?"* "Fine." *"Anything wrong?"* "No. Why?" *"Ever been to Mexico?"* "Nope, never."

"Here, talk to your grandmother. Tell her you're fine and you've never been south of California, willya?"

The scammers counted on her panicking and losing all her fucking sense, and they were right. She would have wired those bastards the money if she hadn't run into Mike. Mike settled for pie and coffee, which is a helluva lot cheaper than 1800 bucks.

I got another lady on my block who is a magnet for every phony salesman in the county. *"Ma'am I notice that your roof is worn at the seams, and will probably leak this spring. That could cause some major damage."* Or … *"there's been an infestation of termites in this neighbor-hood …"*

These guys are worse than congressmen, and they prey on older people who can't go up on the roof and check for themselves. At the end of the block we've got an old guy named Burt (how many Burt-and-Ernie references do you think we get) and he was told there's a big hole in his roof that would cost about a grand to fix it.

So I got out the ladder and went up there myself. Fixed this tiny hole with about a beer glass full of roof patch. Marie wasn't too happy, but Burt sure was. I told Marie, *"Look, if I fall off the roof I promise I will die and not just be paralyzed."* That made her feel better.

And sometimes these bastards are actual, out-and-out burglars --- they want to take the oldster 'in the back to look at the roofline and under the eaves' and while the owner is back behind the house, the partner that they never saw jumps out of the truck and ransacks the living room and the bedrooms.

Scam artists that show up at your door, and the ones that constantly call you on the phone aren't the only ones who piss me off. So do the guys who try to sell you heaven on your visa card. The televangelists.

The ones who don't pay taxes but have six hundred dollar suits, a mansion with 2 private swimming pools, a Rolls Royce and a Bentley. You know who I mean. Some people don't think they belong in this category, but I do.

Still, being smarter than a scam artist doesn't require a master's degree from Harvard. Just because you're old doesn't mean you have to act stupid. And people who are young ... they eventually get frustrated with gray-hairs who act like they've suddenly lost their marbles.

"I don't know if I can do that, maybe you could show me." Meaning, 'maybe you could do it FOR me'. *"I'm not sure how this light bulb goes in, now that they're all twisty."* Seriously? All your life it's been lefty-loosey, righty-tighty; nothing's changed.

Eventually these folks are going to need some real help and they might not get it because they've been asking for all this other shit for years. Sorry for the rant, but for chrissakes, how 'bout a little common sense and effort?

Stamina My stamina left and never said goodbye. I used to love to exercise, to sweat, to stay in shape and have a long rendezvous with the wife. Now, cutting the grass feels like a 10k in August. (Yeah, I cut my own grass; one of the few things I can still do. We'll get to that later).

There're times when I can do one time what I used to be able to do repeatedly– throw a ball, run at a sprint or a jog – at about 60% of my old self. But I sure as hell can't do it twice (ask Marie). My recovery time sucks.

Speaking of Marie, I consider it my duty to make her happy, and it pisses me off that I'm not Mr. Everlast anymore. I used to think foreplay was a waste of time. Not anymore, and it's not just my opinion that's softened. Now I need the foreplay to make up the time.

Marie never complains though; she still treats me like I'm a stud ready for the derby. Sometimes at night it's like prom night and we laugh and have fun being romantic. It's just that the after-prom is a little more ... brief ... than it was 40 years ago. I try my best and a little Korean Red Ginseng helps. But it's not like it was. And she never complains. I married up, way over my head no doubt about it.

One thing about her though---- just when my muscles are going south, Marie changes her travel habits. Whenever we go anywhere her suitcases feel like 5 square feet of liquid mercury. I remember when she packed a Hawaiian shirt and flip-flops and said, "Let's go".

Now she packs everything in the house except the jock itch cream (long story). Yeah, I know the luggage has wheels but you still have to get it in and out of the car 4 times, and the damn wheels twist the suitcase sideways at every crack in the sidewalk.

But aside from sex and traveling (never used that phrase before), one of the things that pisses me off is that I rarely have the stamina to watch all 9 innings of a night game. I close my eyes for just a few seconds during a commercial and the next thing I know it's the 7th inning and 4 runs have scored.

Especially when it's cold out; I sit down, bundle up, grab a beer and cashews, and in the second quarter of the Bears game they cut to some stupid-ass commercial for a car dealer---I swear, every one of them says they're the #1 dealer in the USA—so I rest my eyes. And the next thing

I know it's the 4th quarter and we're down by 14. My beer is warm, my back is stiff and there's a dribble spot on my sweatshirt.

(I know this: the DVR is the best invention since the musical bottle opener.)

I hate losing my stamina like that. I got a lot of friends who gave in; they go to bed at 9 o'clock and get up at 5:00. What in the hell is going on at 5:00 in the morning? Bunch of old fuckers walking around looking like they lost their dog, that's what. And I bite my tongue hard when I see an old couple in matching sweaters ... (*'don't...say...a...word...'*)

Senior This   There's a lot of cutesy old-people phrases that are supposed to make us smile, but most of 'em make me want to go Ralph Kramden on 'em. Just give me the senior discount and don't get cute.

Like when people compliment me and then add "for your age" or a diagnosis begins with "At your age..." Every time I hear that I think 'fuck you'. Once in a while I say it out loud, but I always think it.

Or when I walk in to a room and forget why I came in there; I hear "*senior moment*" whispered behind my back, or "*I'm afraid he's got a serious case of CRS* and there is no cure.*" What, like you never forgot anything?

   * CRS: can't remember shit

One of the things that really pisses me off is that I just thought of a few things that piss me off but by the time I got to the computer I forgot what they are. CRS is a tough disease. Should have written them down, but I couldn't find my reading glasses so I could find a pen.

When I go in to a restaurant with my family I don't want to be a grumpy old fart, and I don't want to be treated like a cute 3rd grader either.

So I figured out how to handle it. Now when a waitress asks me: "Will that be the 'senior' discount? Hee hee hee...I suppose I better ask. Hee hee hee..."

I don't get grumpy anymore. Now I act like I'm going to give a life lesson, and just to give her a taste of her own medicine I guess her to be older than she is.

If the giggling waitress looks to be about 28 I say to her *"look, uh, Christy, you're probably only about 34 so you got a ways to go before you're past your prime like me..."* "34?!! I'm only 28!" *"Really? Well, like you were doing, I'm just going on looks. Anyway, like I was saying...wait, 28? Hmm, I guess waitressing ain't easy. So, Christy ..."* I've never gone past this point because now Marie's jabs to the ribs are starting to feel like Joe Frazier left hooks.

And as long as we're on the subject of restaurants, I gotta tell you, prices have gotten waaay out of hand. No, I'm not some old fart who always wants to tell you that "back in my day" milk was six fucking cents, but damn. Some of these restaurants are competing with colleges to see who can gouge the fastest.

Thirteen bucks for a salad? It's lettuce, garlic cheese and some little blocks of toast for chrissakes. We were out the other night, and a Moretti was eight dollars. Eight dollars. There's a little profit for you. Marie wants to get me a T-shirt that says *"What!?!"* so that every time we get the bill I don't have to yell it out loud.

Pay The Man   Another thing that aggravates me is paying somebody to do work that I should be able to do myself. Climbing a ladder all day and twisting under the eaves like a Cirque du Soleil contortionist never was fun, but I could do it.

Now I pay some young guy and stand back and tell him what he's doing wrong. I suppose I should enjoy surveying the job while someone else does the work; sort of like a king and his subject. *'Make the moat a bit deeper, knave, and change the color scheme on the guillotine.'*

But I don't.

I know a lot of guys use the phrase "I'm too old for that shit." I hate that phrase; I still want to feel 'strong like bull'. But you know what? When it comes to the eaves, or painting the kitchen that takes me three damn days and a half a tube of Ben Gay----I'm too old for that shit.

I'm not talking about cars, though. I didn't get aged out of that one---I got technology-ed out. I open my hood now and it takes me 5 minutes to find the transmission dipstick. What the hell is all this catalytic-sensor-computer-vacuum-cyborg transmogrifier shit? I used to be able to put both arms in my slant 6 and still have room to turn a wrench.

So I don't work on my car anymore; I lost that battle when they got rid of carburetors.

But I still cut my own grass. Some people meditate; I mow the lawn or wash the car. Time to think, relax my mind, do something that I've always known how to do, and accomplish the task at hand. Nothing against the yardmen that everybody else has, but it gives me time to think, and they're usually not the thoughts that piss me off. They're good thoughts. So I got that going for me. Which is nice. (Bill Murray is great.)

Beer Guts and Wives I have a lot of good friends and acquaintances from the team, and from church and the tavern, and it's kind of a sideshow that a lot of guys are in that 51st state---the state of denial. Where they think they are still attractive to young women.

Not just the comb-over guys trying to coax the 17 strands of hair on the east side of their head over to the west side; but the guys that can't walk past a store without stopping to check themselves out in the reflection, and suck in their gut and leer at the women half their age.

The sad truths are: half of these guys couldn't get laid in a whorehouse with a fistful of hundreds. And that's even if they <u>were</u> 20 years younger. And the other half, those guys who looked great 30 years ago …it's two (low) balls and three strikes now.

Even at a wedding when those lovely young ladies are half drunk and wild…. old guys are invisible. Not even on their radar. They'll step on your leering tongue and dance right past you. They ain't interested.

And why would you want them to be? None of us could perform the way those young women would want. That stallion is in our heads--- it ain't any lower than that.

Don't get me wrong; I like the view. I don't care how old I get; when a girl in a summer dress walks by I'm hoping for a strong breeze. But unless you've got a big boatload of money, staring and salivating is all it's gonna be. It's just a spectator sport now.

Inflatable Raft   I guess if they want to suck in their gut and dream that's ok. It's harmless…except when that state of denial rears its head in the direction of their wife. Now, we all kid about our wives, sure, "the old ball-and-chain" stuff or the Rodney Dangerfield "My wife, I'm tellin' ya…."

One time Mike said (too loud) "are you kidding? The closest my wife has come to an orgasm was when she twirled a q-tip too deep in her ear." We laughed until she came over and whacked the back of his head. Then we laughed harder. That's harmless punch-line stuff.

But I don't like it when guys constantly bad-mouth their wife. Complainin' about her and treating her like a second-class citizen.

And most of the guys doin' the bitchin' are no prize either---- a guy whose bowling shirt barely makes it down to his belt buckle 'cause he's got a beergut that looks like he just swallowed a basketball, (a guy you'd look at and say 'hey, when are you due?').

His wife got big after a kid or two, then he says 'fuck it' and he gets the big gut (yeah, I know it could have been the other way around; don't interrupt) and now he's telling us *"Hell, puttin' that wedding ring on her finger was like pullin' the plug on an inflatable raft! Hahaha."*

Yeah, haha. She gets half; enjoy the apartment.

45

High School Idiots   When a guy is an asshat in high school, you kind of understand—he's 15, 16, 17 years old and being influenced by a lot of things that aren't his own choosing.

But when that same guy comes up to you 45 years later and he's still an asshat, that's different. I usually look forward to seeing a lot of the people at my high school reunions, but not all of 'em. Some of 'em make my butt cheeks tighten as I mutter 'oh shit, here it comes'.

Case in point: at my 45 year high school reunion we had a dinner and dance in a hall, then the next day we go down to Lake Michigan for an all-day picnic. Lots of guys are wearing long shirts and hats "to protect from the sun" and embarrassment. I'm going in the water so I take my shirt off, and while I ain't Charles Atlas, I'm ok.

Soon as I do, this jackoff, who could piss off Mother Teresa, points at me and laughs. Now here's a clown who wouldn't know a wrestling mat from a yoga mat, and he yells at me: *"Hey Ernie; looks like you won't be wrestling at 154 any time soon, eh? Hahaha."*

No, I won't be. But he found out that I still got a pretty good take-down. He was shoveling sand out of his ass for half an hour. I strutted away like a rooster coming out of the hen house. My back was killing me but the take-down was worth it.

My old friends liked it too. Lots of us have been friends for over 50 years and no matter how far away we are or how long it's been since we've seen each other, it'll stay like that. And it would have been that way without Facebook too, but with it I can at least keep track of how they're doing.

And I get the added 'pleasure' of having their dinner and their cats and their kids' political views all over my computer screen.

The old political geniuses are on Facebook or bar stools; the younger ones are on twitter or instagram or whatever comes next. At least in a bar you can put your boots up on the foot rail when the shit gets too deep.

Music I like most kinds of music, and it takes me back to where I was and what I was doing when I hear the old songs again. Whether it was Elvis, Frankie Valli, Dino, Sinatra, the Beatles, Stones or even the Doobie Brothers doing 'Black Water'--- Marie would be cooking up Italian beef in the kitchen and I would grab her around the waist and dance, "*I like to hear some funky Dixie Land, pretty mama come and take me by the hand...*"

Back then, like now, most musicians were rebels, but back then they could play. Keith Richards can still play, and while Jimi Hendrix may not have been the poster boy for the United Negro College Fund, he could bend the strings. Some still can---Bruce Springsteen, Jackson Browne, Bonnie Raitt are all great musicians.

I shouldn't say there aren't musicians now. There's a few. The grandkids make me listen to their station when we go anywhere, and I have to admit there's some good music out there---that Bruno Mars kid is great, so is Timberlake.

And Katy Perry could just stand there and I'd watch; she doesn't even have to sing well. But when I pull up to a traffic light it's not Chicago or John Mellencamp blasting at jet-engine decibel level from the next car.

No, those annoying inane, pompous, screaming 'lyrics' mega-bassed at my car with enough force to loosen both the piston rings and the fillings in my teeth come from one type of music: Rap.

The *"Can't Sing and Can't Play So I Strut on Stage and Yell into the Microphone About a Tough Street Life While I Wear A Thousand-Dollar Gold Fucking Chain On My Neck And Have My 'Ho' Drive My Bentley"* kind of rap.

Kids seem to like it when they rapid-fire yell about how they've risen up from the streets to be the powerful, tough individual that will fix the inhumanity in the world. And lots of words rhyme with fuck and bitch an 'ho.

Me? I roll up the windows as fast as I can. In my humble opinion, rap should begin with a "c". Let me sit on my porch with my dog, a beer, and Springsteen or Van Morrison on the box, and I'm pretty happy.

TV Television, however, does not piss me off. If for no other reason than variety, tv is great now. 100 channels, are you kidding me? In HD? What's not to like? I can watch old MASH or Cheers or Hill Street Blues (always liked Renko) or Criminal Minds or The Middle or Tom Harmon's son. I can watch today's baseball game …or the 3rd game of the '78 World Series. And I will watch anything that Ron Howard directs just because he was Opie Taylor. That kid was great.

Back To Traffic Lights Remember when I said I had a story about traffic lights? This isn't a "piss me off" story, but when the traffic shit that does piss me off happens, I'm hesitant to yell at the driver because of something that happened a long time ago.

I was driving my '61 Falcon with my friends, and we stopped at the red light. It turned green and the car in front of us didn't budge. At all. For a while. It just sat there.

Finally the car behind me started honking, and we all leaned out the windows and started yelling "Hey, lady, that's the only shade of green they have!" and "Hey! It's the long pedal!" and "Sometime today! It ain't gonna get any greener!"

The driver leaned over and looked at us with her side rear view mirror. Uh-oh. Then she stepped out. They all stepped out. They were nuns. Our nuns. Angry nuns.

Their car had stalled, and if we didn't help push their huge, heavy Oldsmobile all the way to the service station (past two stations that weren't owned by Catholics) we were all going to hell. So we did.

Thinking of those nuns all those years ago makes me wait just an extra second or two at the intersection.

Speaking of way back when….it pisses me off when I catch myself sometimes reverting back to my childhood. Marie and I sat down late last night and had butterscotch pudding. Pudding. I never had pudding in my teens, 20's, 30's, 40's or 50's but here I am eating pudding. Pretty soon I'll be reverting back to my babyhood and I'll be wearing 'depends'.

I swear if you had told me 25 years ago that I'd be getting up to pee twice a night, forgetting where I put my goddam reading glasses, and have hair growing out of my ears, I'd have said, *"Gas up my '67 T-Bird, put the top down and point me to the nearest cliff. I'll make Thelma and Louise look like amateurs."*

Nah, that's probably not true. I really loved that car. White T with fire-engine red interior. We all have a car in our past that we never should have sold. That was mine.

Sports and Politics   Politics gets talked about a lot around here, with most discussions containing the phrase "those fucking crooks in Washington…"

People take sides and argue their case; ok. I can handle some of these enlightened discussions in the same way I can handle arguments about the Cubs and Sox. Take sides, blow off steam. Sports and politics generate a lot of the same passion, and there're winners and losers.

Political arguments, though, usually end up pissing me off, largely because Congress is a bigger collection of idiots than you'd find at a Phillies game, and the loudmouths who support these unethical morons seem to think that volume equals intelligence.

If you see a picture of the first Continental Congress and see Jefferson, Franklin, Washington, Adams, Hamilton … and then you look at Congress now you'd have to figure that we're going backwards and Darwin was dead wrong.

So when guys want to argue politics ad nauseum I usually shrug and say 'not interested'. And if I have to say it more than once, it's followed by "now shut the fuck up." And if I find out that the jackass doing the arguing didn't even vote in the last election, it's an even bigger "shut the fuck up!" I don't want to hear any complaining from some idiot who didn't even vote.

Am I a liberal, or a conservative? I'm a common sense.

Ernie del Santo

Doesn't seem like too much to ask of a government that we collectively have a social conscience and still be fiscally responsible (see? I went to college.)

I can include myself when I say it's too bad that all the Einsteins who have all the answers to the problems of the world are sitting in cafes or on barstools.

Hope I don't trip getting off this soapbox.

Oh no! An ethnic joke I have mixed feelings about political correctness though. Hate-speech is bullshit and I won't listen to it. But I miss telling jokes that are just jokes, and it pisses me off that I have to watch myself even if I'm telling an Italian joke.

If I'm at the bowling alley and I tell Felipe '*hey, you know why Puerto Ricans have such trouble with checking accounts? 'Cuz the checks are too small to spray-paint their names on!*' and he comes back with "*you know those Italian snow tires? Dago through mud, dago through snow, but when dago flat dago wop wop wop.*'

C'mon, you know this one: what's the difference between an Irish wake and an Irish wedding? How about this one: what happens in East Texas when somebody gets hit with either a tornado or a divorce? You know the punch lines. They're jokes with no vitriol, and if a guy can't tell a joke without hurting somebody then he's a bad joke teller at best, or an asshole at worst. End of sermon.

I have a lot more patience for sports arguments. I like that guys get passionate about their teams and players and sometimes there's agreement with stats to back it up: 'this guy can't hit his weight, that goalie is tough as nails, this pitcher couldn't find the strike zone with a GPS...''

Sometimes it's therapeutic. Lots of guys I know have trouble talking to their dads, or their brothers. Hatchets that haven't been completely buried.

But they can always talk sports. They can always watch a game together. Here's my advice to older guys who have had 'disagreements' with their kids --- re-connect by going to your grandson's Little League or Pop Warner games or soccer matches. Watch and cheer, don't judge. Be the old guy you wish was around when you were playing. That's Dr. Ernie's advice. Pay at the door.

But while we're on sports, do I think the pro players make too goddam much money and the tickets are too high? Yeah. But I love sports and can talk it all day.

And even though sometimes I may argue my point, I never, ever get mad about opposing points of view on sports. EXCEPT.....One time I remember getting 'annoyed'. Pissed off, you might say; enough that I still remember the details even though it was about 1993.

I was in an airport bar in O'Hare waiting for Marie to come back from her sister's, and above the Bushmills and

Wild Turkey shelf was a big tv with a pro basketball game on.

And speaking of turkeys, a couple of guys from Miami come in and sit down next to me. And one of them looks at the tv for 2 seconds and starts going on and on about this kid on the Miami Heat, Harold Minor. I ignore him. He then says that Minor is better than Michael Jordan.

I turned to him, could see that he was an idiot, and turned away. He touches my shoulder and says to me *"I'm right, right? Did you see that dunk? Harold Minor is going to make everybody forget there ever was a Michael Jordan, you know?"*

I said "I can't talk basketball with you" and turned away. He says, *"Oh, you don't know anything about basketball?"* That's it.

I wheel on him. "No, YOU don't. You don't know shit about the game of basketball. Jordan will go down as the best player we've ever seen, offensively AND defensively, and Minor won't be in the top two hundred. The game is about more than just dunks. Preach to your friends. Maybe they don't think you're a fucking idiot." I turned away again.

He started to get really pissy and wanted to argue some more but I never turned his way again. His friends finally pulled him away to another part of the bar.

I got nothing against Harold Minor; probably a nice guy; had a good college career. But to compare him to Jordan was stupid. I doubt that anybody in Miami would listen to that asshole's argument, but we were in Chicago. You don't talk shit about Jordan here.

If he would've started bagging on Walter Payton we probably would have gotten into a fight.

Speaking of Minor   There are other minor little things that piss me off, but no big deal. Like in certain parts of my legs the veins look like a road map of the Baja. Or when I take a quick nap on my back I have to reach down and pull my balls out from in-between my legs. I don't remember them hanging so low and me having to do that when I was young.

One time I did that, and I didn't know little Maggie Marie had just walked in the room. *"What are you doing, Grandpa?"* Oh, hi, I was just….checking gravity. *"Gravity?"* Yup, testicular gravity. And everything is where it's supposed to be. *"That's good, isn't it?"* Yup. So let me rest now ok? Come and get me after 4 songs".

She put her headphones back on and left. And it must not have made an impression on her because I didn't hear anything about it from Beth. And I would have.

Other little things piss me off, but when I think of them I'm in another part of the house, and by the time I get over to the keyboard to write 'em down I forgot what the

Ernie del Santo

hell they were. I said that once, didn't I? Oh well. But I don't have any problem remembering this next one….

Big Print and Little Glasses   I may sound like a whiney prick here, but I hate reading glasses.

Absolutely hate 'em. I got about six pairs and I can never find any of 'em.

I thought I read my last "big-word book" when I was in the third grade, but when I can't find my glasses I curse every font under 16.

And for chrissakes, there isn't anybody with an age under Butkus' number that reads the newspaper anymore anyway. So why in the hell don't they make the print bigger? (Butkus was number 51; you knew that, right? Find me somebody under the age of 51 who reads a real newspaper).

I need arms the length of a '73 Cadillac just to check the box scores or see how much money I lost in the stock market.

Actually it's not the glasses that annoy me; anybody can need glasses at any age. Kids wear glasses. But *'reading'* glasses? Fuhgetaboutit --- that just means you're old. And bifocals? Bifocals are supposed to be for a librarian, a great-grandmother or a defense secretary.

When I was in high school I got called in to the principal's office a lot, and he would sit me down to have a "chat". But when he leaned on his desk, looked down at me over his little half-glasses I thought he was the oldest man working and I stopped paying attention. Everything he said after that sounded like slow-speed feedback through an amplifier.

But as much as I hate the damn glasses, my appendages don't reach so far anymore, so when I grab the newspaper I grab my specs—if I can find 'em.

Speaking of reading -- and this probably belongs in some other section but I'm thinking of it now and if I don't write it down I'll forget it – my dad used to take a magazine into the bathroom and sit down on the toilet for half an hour and read.

When I was young I never understood that. First of all, we only had one bathroom in the house, so it was a pain for the rest of us. (Me and Vinnie made a lot of brown spots in the backyard grass. Both of us thought *"shit or get off the pot "* was a literal phrase).

Second, he had a hundred-dollar Lazy-Boy in the living room, why sit on a cracked 4-dollar toilet seat and read?

Now I get it. Only took me 50 years. My dad had intestinal problems and needed to be in there. And he died young. Every day I wish he'd been around longer; every day I feel that loss.

Ernie del Santo

And I hope my kids feel the same way about me, so I'm gonna take care of myself for as long as I can, and that includes those damn check-ups. Keep reading; you'll see what I mean.

"The best doctor in the world is the veterinarian. He can't ask his patients what is the matter. He's got to just know."

- Will Rogers

Ernie del Santo

© Tom Cain

COLONOSCOPY MY ASS

One of the more disturbing aggravations of getting old is having a very young-looking 36 year old doctor look up from your medical chart and say "*You know, AT YOUR AGE, you really need to have some very invasive, painful, embarrassing and expensive tests done, some of which will involve shoving tubes the size of an industrial shop-vac hose up your anal cavity and all through your torso so we can look for cancers and pieces of a fried baloney sandwich that you ate in the 7ᵗʰ grade.*"

I've probably spent more time and money in the doctor's office in the last two years than I did in the previous twenty years. I always believed the old saying that '*if you go and do what the doctor says, your illness will be over in 6 or 7 days; if you don't go, it could take a week.*'

But now I have to go, and I've made a lot of his Mercedes payments with check-ups, a broken toe, a shot for shingles, blood pressure tests, a chunk of who-knows-what removed from my skin, flu shot…and I haven't even been sick!

Most of the time I'm just trying to prevent the crap that keeps happening to my friends---like stents in the heart and cancer treatments.

You remember when I talked about my dad? Intestinal problems weren't his only thing. By the time he went to the doctor for that there wasn't much they could do.

He died of cancer and it was tough to watch. My big strong dad reduced to a shell of himself. He went early, too early; would have loved to grow old with him. He missed a lot of things that I don't want to miss.

You know the old saying 'one day we will die, but all the other days we won't'? If I want to get through all the 'other days' I gotta take care of my insides. Cancer is a nasty, unforgiving bastard that's taken too many of my relatives and friends, and the same goes for heart attacks.

Standing over my buddy's hospital bed right after he got a stent put in his artery is a real reminder to cut down on the fried shit that we like to eat. (We won't even talk about the hospital bills; that'll be later. Six bucks for an aspirin for chrissakes.)

So anyway, I'm going in to have them check me out for colon cancer again. This will be my second one. And let me tell you—if you think a prostate exam is rough, you might want to double up on the anesthetic for this one.

But I don't want to die because I'm afraid, or too stupid to let them shove a tube up where no man has gone before (trust me on that). So here I go.

This time, though, things will be different. I'll be knocked out. Not like the last time.

My First Colonoscopy   Twelve years ago I was in my 50's, and still feeling pretty good about my physical condition. The week before the colonoscopy 'procedure' the doc and I were talking about the stuff you have to drink (that vat of industrial waste that makes you stay within 10 feet of the porcelain) and the fasting.

Then he started telling me about the actual process, the tools they use—the camera, the light and the forceps-type thing, and how he would watch the whole thing on a tv screen as he was doing it.

It sounded interesting, kind of like the Magic School Bus cartoon that the kids used to watch, where they'd miniaturize themselves and zoom through the body and discover things. I thought 'what the hell, if it's going to be right there on a tv set, I want to see it too'.

So I told him I wanted to be awake and watch as he does it. He said no, you don't do that, he has to knock me out, he can tell me all about when I wake up, blah blah blah.

I was about to let it go, until he said, *"Besides, if you were to be awake there would be no anesthetic of any kind and you probably couldn't handle the pain."*

Excuse me? I can't handle it? *"Well, it's not just that, but yes, it is painful and as we get up in years we try to keep the pain at a minimum."*

Up in years, huh? All of his degrees are on the wall behind him, and I don't give a shit. I tell him "I can handle pain and I want to see it." He tries again to talk me out of it---apparently he's only had one other person awake during a colonoscopy, and that was another colonoscopy doctor---and I'm still pissed off that this young sonuvabitch said I wasn't tough enough.

So I make him a deal. I tell him if he lets me watch the whole thing and talk to him during it, I'll write it all down and get it into the local newspaper. People will read it and be encouraged to get the thing that might save them from the most preventable cancer there is (I read that in his brochure).

And he agreed. I couldn't tell if he was hoping for some publicity or if he just wanted to see if I would break. I walked out of his office feeling triumphant ... for about ten seconds. What in the hell did I just do? Well, it was done, so I'll prepare and I'll have a story to tell. Marie thought I was being an idiot. And she's usually right about these things.

The prep made me feel like I was getting ready for a boxing match, drinking my food and cutting weight. He said I had to fast completely for 24 hours; I decided to make it 30 because I wanted to see a smooth tube up there, not the brown remains of yesterday's pasta.

When I got there they must have seen some trepidation in my eyes 'cause they asked me again if I wanted to be awake. I have to admit they were really kind and accommodating; I think we were all curious ... for different reasons.

They wheeled me down to the room with the tools and the television (big mother up on the wall) and I was lying on my side with my rear end exposed. I forgot about the fact that they were all female nurses.

Then as she takes her long gloved fingers and puts the cold lube up my bottom I start reconsidering my braggadocio. First thought: '*My gawd what did I get myself in to...*' Then came the tube.

At this point, and throughout this discussion, let me make this point about having absolutely no anesthetic and being awake—NEVER DO THIS.

Ok, back to the 'procedure'. So they grab the tube and insert it; I could feel my eyes bulge out of my skull, and a squeal flew out of my open mouth; I'm ready to scream but I don't. I feel it going in to my body and making a slight turn—feel every inch.

I look at the nurse in front of me and she's smiling. So I grunt, "*I would never do well in prison*" and grit my teeth.

She laughs, and I think the doctor did too but he was behind me and I had no interest in looking back.

I feel the tube go around my rib cage and I can see it on tv. For a brief moment I forgot about the pain and just watched myself on tv. I looked good on the inside. "Great preparation Mr. del Santo." *"Thanks. I fasted a little longer so you could see what you're looking for."* "Very thoughtful," he said as he rammed the tube harder.

A minute later I hear him struggling and I feel it in my torso. What an odd sensation. I look up at the tv and I can see what I'm feeling. "We're making a turn, here, around your rib cage. Just having a bit of trouble turning the corner."

A 'bit of trouble'? Damn. I said I was tough, I didn't say I was Superman. I grit my teeth. He asks, "Does this hurt?" I think 'hell yes it hurts!' So I tell him. *"Nah."*

He finally makes the goddam turn and the tube snakes through me as I watch on tv until – uh oh. Suddenly my tunnel doesn't look so smooth. His voice drops a little, "Ahh. Do you see that? That's a polyp."

I see it. A cancer polyp? Damn. But before I can panic he says it's probably benign but he'll have to remove it. I see the forceps come out of the tube, GRAB the polyp and RIP it out. And I feel every tug inside my gut.

Again, what a strange sensation; ripping out a piece of my insides while I watch on tv; a bit of an out-of-body experience. Any moment now I think the Alien is going to jump out of my chest.

He didn't find any more, and soon he hit the end of the line. I was damned relieved to feel the tube going backwards through my body. I think that's the closest I will ever be to feeling what it's like to give birth.

A big sigh of relief at the end; I made it through. The nurse who took a few pictures during the procedure showed them to me and the other nurses. Glad I was good for a laugh.

After the post-op the Dr. sees Marie and Michael in the waiting room, *"Ah, here's the reason we do what we do."* They gave me a hug and asked, "How are you feeling?"

"Never better," I lied. I walked out with my head held high and my legs wide apart like a cowboy who'd spent the last 8 hours in a saddle. I don't think my farts made any sound for a day and a half.

And now, looking back on it, it was amazing. Once. I'll never do it that way again. This time when I go in I'm going to take every anesthetic I can and say "nightly-night, wake me up when it's done."

I'm glad I saw it; glad I know what it's about. But sequels are never as good as the original (except for Godfather II) so I'll sleep through this one.

CAVEAT: Do not, let me repeat, DO NOT complain to your wife about a colonoscopy. Don't bitch about the tube, feeling invaded, oh the diarrhea and the pain, or any of that bullshit. When it comes to having things shoved up into your body or pulled out of your private parts, women are the champs.

Soon as they hear you whine you'll get that arched eyebrow and that look of "oh, they shoved something inside of you and it hurt? Welcome to the club, sissy." And that'll be just the beginning. Spare yourself. Keep your dignity.

Teeth   Enough about my ass, let's move to the other side. And as long as we're talking about anesthetics and toughness...

The older I get the worse my teeth are.   Lot of bad habits that I use my mouth to do. Chewing gum, coffee, and the fact that my parents never bought floss when I was a kid; never knew it existed, so I had a few cavities at an early age.

Now I've got caps, bridges, an implant and an old gold crown from 1981. I was at the dentist not too long ago, and I told him my back molar hurt. He took a quick look and said it's got to come out. "Way too infected" to be saved, and "you don't need it."

He doesn't do extractions, but the guy two doors down does. So he calls and the guy has an opening now. Right now. That should have been a red flag right there.

I'm supposed to pick up Marie in a half hour, but it hurts and he's available so I say, *"let's do it."* I go down the hall, he shoots me with novocaine and gets the dental pliers. But I can still feel everything, so he sticks my gum with another shot. Five minutes later, another. This has happened to me before where the painkiller didn't work. We wait ten more minutes. Still no numbness.

Finally, I said what is probably the stupidest thing I've ever said in my life: *"Just pull it doc. I'm tough, I can take it."* You'd think I'd learn.

Dr. Yankoff stretches my mouth open as wide as it can go (and I feel his hand bracing on my lip so I know right then that the anesthetic still isn't working), puts his yanking tool in there and in the next 5 seconds I had never had so much concentrated pain in such a small area in my life.

I yelped like a first-grade girl, a tear streamed down each cheek --- it felt like he put a Dirty Harry .44 Magnum in my mouth and pulled the trigger.

Blood was flying and rolling down my throat. Then he leaned in to me and whispered, *"I have bad news. I didn't get it all."* Oh, Christ, here we go again. In went the .44 Magnum -- boom! – and after he yanked it out he shoved a big wad of gauze in my mouth.

He handed me two other wads of gauze and I needed 'em as I drove off. Of course Marie sees the bloody gauze in her cup holder and asks, *"What happened to you?!"* "What happened? Well, I was in this saloon, and this guy with a gun calls me a pussy, so…….."

The colonoscopy was dumb, but at least I learned some things. This *"I'm tough, I can take it"* with the dentist was just fucking stupid.

One Pill Makes You Larger When I was growing up my grandparents had pill boxes---several boxes in a row, or, like my grandpa's, a long one with the initials of the days of the week stamped on it. And they took these pills every day for various maladies; my guess was that the Thursday and Friday pills cured the side effects of the Sunday and Monday pills.

Marie and I are both older than my grandparents were when they died, but we hardly take any medicines, save for the ibuprofen when I do painfully stupid activities. We're very lucky. Most older folks have to take one or more … arthritis medicine, insulin, heart medicine, something.

I don't have to take blood thinners; I can usually find time to get my recommended two or three alcoholic drinks per week. But I feel for the people who are taking all kinds of medications. Never met one that didn't have side effects.

"Zits and gray hair on the same face just ain't right."

- Vinnie del Santo

"...and watch the smoke drift up to the heavens."

THE FIVE ACES

Thursday night. Five of us. Old guys. Legends in our own minds. The Five Aces, defending champions of the Senior B league, stride in to the alley and knock the crap out of the pins. Most times. Some nights we couldn't knock 'em over with a baseball bat, but hey…

When the Aces get together, at least once a night we laugh so hard we hurt, just like when we were kids. That's why I play.

A while back my friend Howard, Jewish guy, (what?) asked me and a couple of my old softball friends to join a bowling league. He has a real estate company called Ace Realty that would sponsor us, so me, Howard, my brother Vinnie, Lumpy and Reggie formed our team.

We ended up naming the team after his real estate company. Howard stinks as a bowler, but he pays the league fees and buys the shirts, so we're the Five Aces. Besides, "Four Catholics and a Jew" wouldn't fit on the back of the shirt.

Reggie Watkins is our anchor, our number 1 bowler. He's been a cop for 40 years, retires next year. He's fun to watch---no finesse to his game, all power. He just throws the ball a hundred miles an hour down the middle and hopes for the best. Cracked more than a few pins over the years.

Reggie likes being a cop, likes being out on patrol and he's worked a lot of night-shifts. To amuse himself, he sometimes would do impersonations when he pulled a car over and asked for the license and registration. Usually Samuel Jackson (*...so lemme ask you: 'what's in your wallet?'*), Eddie Murphy or Darth Vader.

One night Reggie and his partner see a car going a little too fast and tailgating down Lake Shore Drive so he pulls the guy over, mostly to see if he'd been drinking. Reggie gets his big frame out of the patrol car, and as he walks up he starts doing Sylvester Stallone: *'Hey, yo Mick, you drive that fast you gotta leave a gap, you know? You got gaps, I got gaps, everybody that ever stepped in the ring's got gaps. C'mon Mick, gimme your license'.*

Reggie stood back very pleased with his impersonation. Then the guy rolls his window down and launches in to Burgess Meredith: *'Rocky, you wanna beat this bum you gotta train like a champion! You gotta eat lightning and crap thunder! Now start hitting that bag like you mean it! And remember: Women weaken legs!'*

Reggie just stood there and laughed. "I couldn't give this guy a ticket, he did a better Mickey than I did Rocky." Reggie handed him a warning, and the guy finished with *"You're a good cop, kid; you got heart. But you need a manager. A manager."* And he drove off.

I love that story. A few weeks after he told it, Marie and I got a dog and we named him Rocky Balboa.

Lumpy Lewandowski I've known since 6th grade. His real name is Larry, Lawrence Joseph Lewandowski, but I've never heard anyone call him that. He's always been Lumpy. My dad had a friend when I was growing up, Porky Portlach. Knew him all my life; I have no idea what his real name is.

Lumpy is a CPA and does all of our taxes. The Lump finds every deduction and then some; takes your tax return right to that red flag line and then backs it off an inch. Model of consistency as a bowler too. Over the past eight years he has averaged either 170 or 171, every year. I got a story about him that I'll tell you later.

Vinnie is my brother, and that alone makes him an Ace; family is family. Vinnie is a natural and would be a great bowler if he would 'apply himself' as the nuns used to tell him. But that ain't Vinnie. The worker gene never made it down to my brother.

F.L. Club   We all know a guy like Vinnie. Life-long member of the F.L. club. Fucking Lucky club. You know guys like that, right? Could fall in shit and come out smelling like a rose. Vinnie doesn't work too hard, doesn't play by the established rules, and he does just fine. A couple of months ago Vinnie said he was going to retire soon, and there was a collective *"from what?!?"* heard throughout the alley.

One time, years ago, he was down in Atlanta and he was hitting on this girl he met in a café. They started dating. Vinnie had a little money from a traffic accident settlement down there, where the other person's insurance company paid twice what his heap was worth and then paid his 'pain and suffering' (see what I mean about the luck?)

Anyway, this girl worked at a hardware store there that was going to go public with their stock, and told Vinnie he should buy some. He just wanted to get in her pants, and he had a little money in his, so he did. And that hardware store went public. Little place called Home Depot. He lived on that for a good long while.

Holy Rollers   About six months ago we were playing the Holy Rollers and Vinnie was due up. As Vinnie was getting his ball, a guy sitting at the scorer's table asked me if I knew Roy, the Holy Rollers' next bowler. Roy had been gone a while, and came back a lot thinner.

The scorer didn't know it, but I'd known Roy for 30 years, so I set him up for a punch line. *"Do I know him? Hell, Roy is like a brother to me!"*

And right on cue Roy spins around and yells *"Ernie, I've met your brother. Fuck you!"* Vinnie turns around, *"Hey!"* highly insulted, and proceeds to roll one of his few strikes of the night. Roy yells back, *"You're welcome."* I bought him a vodka for that one and we laughed like third graders.

Roy was a good guy, considering he was a lawyer. Helluva competitor; told the worst jokes. I say 'was' because last week was in fact his last. Roy had cancer, thought he had beat it---that's when he came back to the league---but it reared its nasty head and came back. Roy passed last Tuesday.

Way too often lately we have to do the ritual that we do. I put on my best shirt, iron my pants, grab my sport coat and go down to the cigar store and grab another box of coronas. I think we're keeping that store in business; this ritual is becoming way more regular than any of us want.

Whenever a friend or a competitor passes, we go to the funeral home, pay our respects to the man and his family, then we go out to the grass near the parking lot and I pass out the coronas.

Ernie del Santo

We light them up and watch the smoke drift up to the heavens. Very few words are spoken. Just the smoke, sailing higher and higher.

We miss our friend, and think about our own mortality. Last week it was Roy. Who knows who will be next? Could be any one of us. That feeling is thicker than the smoke from twelve cigars.

Back To The Alley   Aside from Marie, my best friends are in the bowling league. I don't know what I'd do without my friends. We laugh and have a good time every week and I always look forward to Thursday night, even if I've been bowling shitty the past few weeks.

Last year when we were trying to hold on to first place, Howard was having a terrible game. The rest of us were doing ok; in fact Reggie was throwing a 220, so it didn't matter much. But Howard is a worrier and fretted every missed spare.

So in the 7th frame of the final he decides to change his game. Change his strategy. He grabs Reggie's ball---a ball that looks puny when Reggie holds it but next to Howard's 155-lb. body it looked really big---and Howard is determined to throw like Reggie. He's gonna speed up to the foul line and throw it with all his might (such as it is), just like Reg.

78

Ok, we nod as straight-faced as we can; let's see it. Howard stands there, steely-eyed, staring at the pins, then starts. He winds up, swings the ball behind him as he moves, grunts, and with all the force in his body he flings the ball down the lane .... just ahead of **his teeth** that also go spinning down the alley. He threw it so hard his dentures flew out.

Howard ran down the lane to make sure the pinsetter didn't crush 'em, while the rest of us fell over laughing. Vinnie yells, "*Let 'em go, they might actually knock a pin down for ya!*" The guys on the Southside Lounge gave him another roll just for the comedy of it all. The dentures were dirty, so we soaked 'em in whiskey "to disinfect 'em".

We won the league so we took a pair of toy choppers and glued 'em to the ball on his trophy. He still has it in his office. There is comedy in getting old.

I started to tell you about Lumpy earlier but I got distracted. The Lump, as I said, is a straight-forward numbers guy, in life and in bowling. No surprises; he's an accountant for chrissakes, what you see is what you get. Or so we thought.

Now, usually on Thursday nights in the lounge at the bowling alley there's a small band that gets together and plays. Couple of guitars and a drum set. Nice, not great but better than nothing. The Hip Replacements.

One night a few years back, they don't show up; one of their wives was very sick I think. I guess we didn't realize how much we liked having them around until the one night they weren't.

We were talking about having live music in the background, so Lumpy sees a guitar behind the bar, picks it up, tunes it, and sits on the stool in front of the mike. *"Let's start with 'City of New Orleans'. You guys remember Steve Goodman and Arlo Guthrie?*

My jaw dropped to the floor like if Sofia Vergara had just walked in. In all the time I knew him, Lumpy had never once mentioned that he played guitar. And he was good.

He played for about 25 minutes, then needed to 'lubricate' his throat. Sometimes, you just don't know.

Last thing on the Aces See if you can visualize this: In 2013 Halloween fell on a Thursday night, our bowling night. So we went to the alley dressed as KISS. Five old clowns dressed in leather and make-up, Lumpy with his electric guitar and Reggie bringing up the rear with a boombox on his shoulder playing "***I…want to rock and roll all nii-iight. And party every day***" with all of us marching in and singing it.

Marie still has nightmares over that one. You should have seen the grandkids faces when they saw that video.

*I was in line at the supermarket with this young
'lady' behind me talking on her cell phone. Since I
was hearing the whole damn conversation anyway, I
thought I'd turn around and see who was talking.
Then the girl with the tattoos, Marlboros and
Absolut says into the phone, "This old man is looking
at me. Creeping me out."*

*So I told her, "You'll be old yourself someday."
Then I looked her up and down and changed my
mind: "...on second thought, probably not."*

*When I turned back around and moved my groceries
up the old clerk gave me a wink.*

I didn't think I was that loud.

THINGS I DO

Remember when I told you earlier that this book wouldn't be just a bitch-session about getting old? Ok, so I bitched a bit, sue me. But getting old sucks and now that I'm deep into the back nine of my life there's some things I have to do to get by.

Take It From Dr. Ernie Every day for 20 seconds each, I stand on one leg. Balance is as critical to old guys as it is to a boat and I don't want to capsize. I know too damn many people that look like the kids' clown punching bag with the sand in the bottom-—one false move and down they go. They eventually pop back up, but with an artificial hip. I have enough trouble with my half-jog/half-walk without a broken hip added to the mix. Imagine how cranky I would be with a broken hip.

I'm no gymnast, but after a shower while I'm toweling off I keep pretty balanced on the one leg, and ready to switch to the other leg quickly. So if something ever does knock into me or I trip on a damn dog toy that was left in the hallway, I have enough equilibrium to recover without hitting the floor broadside.

I don't want a plastic hip; I know that Bo Jackson had an artificial hip when he played for the White Sox, but I ain't Bo Jackson, and my bowling is bad enough as it is.

To keep it strong I still exercise and do roadwork. Sort of. My roadwork now is a combination of walking and running. And I take my dog, Rocky Balboa, with me most mornings. We both need the exercise and he needs to get out of the house. But like every frickin' dog, just as I get a good pace going he has to stop and investigate a smell.

The first four or five times I indulge him, but after that I tug on the leash and say *"C'mon! It's old piss for chrissakes, let's go!"*

But instead of actually listening to the guy who buys his dog chow, he pulls back and looks at me like he's Detective Philip Marlowe. *"Wait ... sniff sniff ... Dachshund ... sniff sniff ... 18 pounds ... sniff sniff sniff... Alpo. No, Purina."*

"Alright already! Let's go!!!" I sound like Ralph Kramden yelling at Ed Norton.

Ready to Run   Another thing I do is sleep in gym shorts and a t-shirt. If a disaster happens, I am ready to run out in to the street unembarrassed.

Every year somebody buys me boxer shorts with cute-ass sayings on them (a happy face with its tongue out and 'come and get it' printed on the crotch slot) or some god-awful pajamas. And every year I throw them in the closet and that's where they stay.

If there's a fire or a tornado and I have to run out of the house in the middle of the night, I'll look like I'm going out to shoot hoops, not looking like a birthday-party clown. That'll be my brother Vinnie. He loves that goofy shit, and it makes it easy for Marie at Christmas.

Vinnie will go out to get the newspaper in a dago-T and boxer shorts with the Rolling Stones mouth and tongue on the crotch slot, then stand there and read the paper to make sure the ladies across the street see him. I guess it is funny.

Blood Sucker   I still give blood at the local hospital. Have been doing it for years for the simple reason that it helps, and giving it doesn't affect me. Never did. I could give blood in the afternoon, drive home and cut the grass in the evening. So why not?

I figure that sometime, somewhere, somebody is gonna get splattered all over the pavement and need some blood. They'll get a pint of my A-negative, be instantly revived, and go on to do great things … all the while wondering… *'why do I cuss so much now?'*

Quick story: you know how, when you're going to give blood, they have to screen you first. They put you in a small office and ask a lot of standard questions.... 'Are you in good health? Any heart problems, are you on any medication?' and then two questions... 'Have you paid for sex in the last 3 years? And have you had sex with a man in the last 3 years?'

I probably shouldn't, considering this is a hospital, but I can't help but have fun with these. When the lady asked, "Have you paid for sex?" I've always answered, "*YES, it costs a fortune; I've been married for 38 years and I've paid thousands.*" (her eyebrows arch up and look at me sideways). "*Oh, did you mean <u>directly</u> paid for it? No, but indirectly it's pretty damn expensive. I think I could've had a hooker every night for less.*"

She asked several health questions in her standard monotone and then came to: '*Have you had sex with a man in the last 3 years?*'

The lady was large, maybe in her late 40's, but I could see a spark in there so I said, "*No, ... have you?*"

Again with the arched eyebrow. She asked about four more questions in her monotone, then leaned in to me and said very definitely "*And yes, I have.*"

I enjoyed that more than my own jokes.

But the real killer was one time when they had a guy doing the questions. Thin black guy (what?) with glasses.

Seemed like a nice guy, one I could joke with, so after asking me about 15 ailments that I never heard of, I asked him, *"Hey, do you know why PMS is called 'PMS'?"*

He said no. *"Because Mad Cow Disease was already taken!"* He laughed loud enough to have the staff wonder what the hell was going on in there.

So, 15 minutes later I'm in the blood donor room full of female nurses, I got the squeeze ball in my hand, the wrap around my arm and a nurse just about to stick the needle in my vein and draw blood.

As she's standing over me, with said needle, that same guy that I was joking with bursts in to the room and says, "There he is! Hey, you wanna hear the joke this guy just told me?"

Not now, ya knucklehead! I motion to him, then say, *"Not the best time, there's a needle pointing at me."* He tells the PMS joke as loud as he can, then laughs like a hyena.

The nurse's eyes get big and full of mischief. *"Oh, this guy told you that, did he? Well, I might just miss that big old vein of his, you know?"* I did a verbal tap dance as best I could but this is the first time the needle ever hurt.

Afterwards they offered me cookies and juice, but I didn't trust 'em. It was like the witch offering food to Hansel and Gretel, so I stayed away.

Saving Face   A couple of things that I do have to do with my face in the morning. No, I don't mean taking a razor to it; shaving has nothing to do with old age. It sucks at any age. Except for the very first time you shave. That's the only time it's cool.

I use moisturizer on my face every day, for the same reason I used to put oil on my baseball glove. Gotta keep the old leather pliable and looking shiny. And my skin is looking pretty good, smooth as the pavement in front of the mayor's house. I hope that someday someone asks me if I ever had 'work done'. I'll say, "*Yeah, I've had my face worked on,*" and then tell them about the bar fight at the Wild Hare back in my 20's. So far no one's asked.

The other face thing has to do with my foul mouth, and I don't mean my charming turn of the profane phrase. I mean the germs and stains.

I know guys who wouldn't let their 2006 Buick get dirty, but their teeth look like the hill-jack's in 'Deliverance'.

After my breakfast and coffee ... and sometimes I like to put blueberries on my cereal and those little blue bastards can really throw a stain ... I have to brush and really swish that mouthwash around. I mentioned before that I have caps and crowns, a bridge on my top teeth and an implant. (Most of us old guys do ... if we're lucky. If a guy isn't lucky, his teeth are like Howard's and sit in a jar at night).

When you have bridges, there's spaces between the porcelain and the gums, and where there's spaces there's places for food to hide. And if that food gets under there and stays for a while, your breath smells like a bar rag at midnight. So I have to put the floss through that little fishing line loop and get up under there.

———————

I remember when I was a kid working at the local Walgreens and there were those old guys who always wanted to get close to you, like they had a secret, and then they tell you how you should run your life. Half the time they smelled like cigarettes and stale beer; the other half it was worse.

That memory stays with me; there was one old guy named Shorty Firestone. Couldn't forget his name: *"Firestone! You know the tire company?"* He'd puff out his chest like he was heir to the fortune... *"No relation! Hahaha."*

He would get *thisclose* to me with his philosophies on work ethic and race and I swear I'd almost faint. His breath smelled like liver, cigars and yesterday's gin. I don't want to put my grandkids through that.

Just ask the little brats if your breath stinks; they'll tell you. I'm a grandpa that likes to get right up next to the kids, partly so that I can whisper untruths in their ears without their parents hearing me, and because I like to mess with 'em.

But if I have bad breath they will lean back like they just got a big whiff of sour milk, scrunch up their face and whine: *"Grandpa your breath smells like dog doo-doo!"* Then mom or dad comes in and scolds them for their brutal honesty and you become bad grandpa. You don't want that.

[However, if you have a streak of wicked in you and want to gross out your grandkids, cough up phlegm in front of them. Even if it's into your napkin. And when they go *"Eeww! Yuck!"* just whisper to them mischievously, "wanna see it?"]

Stress Remember *"illegitimus non carborundum est."*? Well, sometimes the bastards do grind you down. Whether it's traffic, or the internet geek on the phone from 6-thousand miles away who can't figure out how to tell you he has no fucking idea what's wrong with your service, or just little aggravations around the house like the flapper that you just replaced leaks again ... you need an outlet.

Mine is a basketball hoop. I originally put it up in the backyard for the kids, but when I was manager at the post office branch, I started using it as my therapy. And when all the things that piss me off at work or in general (previous chapter) get to me, 5 minutes of shooting gets me back to my charming loveable self.

A few lay-ups, a few three-pointers, a couple of jump shots, a fade-away and then I drive the lane on Bill Walton. Beat him every time. A little sweat, and it clears the head.

If I'm not at home and the bastards are out in force, I have to chew gum to get rid of the anxiety. I know, maybe that's part of the reason my teeth are terrible, but it has its advantages.

When I was in about 5th grade I read a book about Jack Dempsey, the boxer. He used to chew gum to strengthen his jaw so that he could take a hit. Made sense to me, so I started chewing gum.

Now I don't really need a stronger jaw, but I still chew gum because there are times when I just find that my jaw is clenched for no particular reason. I'll be fixing a bowl of cereal and realize my jaw is tight or my teeth are grinding.

And way too often I'm in my car and somebody throws trash out the window of the car next to me or runs a red light, and my teeth gets clenched. Next thing you know, it hurts. The gum relaxes and works out the jaw. So when I'm driving I have a pack in the console. 'Cause there's a lot of bastards out there.

Crime and Punishment Somewhere around 1978, I made a decision about drinking. A lot of my friends drank too much and I was slowly turning into one of them. Guys go out after work for a drink or two, two becomes three, and next thing you know it's "holy crap, I've got to get home!" I had kids and a wife that were counting on me. And a good job, and I didn't want to show up at the post office smelling like yesterday's Peroni.

So I made a decision to cut down to just the one week night that we played ball, to cut myself off early, and thatevery night I drank, I would get up in the morning and run it off.

No matter how early I had to get up, if I did the crime, I had to do the punishment. It only takes a few of those jogs in the early morning with your head pounding and beer streaming out of every pore in your body to say "that's it."

Marie and I still have a glass of wine together, and I'll still have one or two on bowling night, but ever since 1978 I've tried to follow the old coach Knute Rockne's advice: *"Drink the first, sip the second, skip the third."*

Left-Handed Day When I was pretty young my dad broke his right arm at work. He was in a cast for about a month, and during that month he had to learn how to do things with his left hand. That was probably the month I learned all the ways to use cuss words.

He had such a rough time with it, I decided to have a left-handed day every month or so. I would try to do everything with my left hand that day – write, eat, button my shirt. I swear I thought brushing my teeth would be the easiest; who knew my left wrist had to be taught to twist around like that?

I developed a pretty good left-handed hook shot, and can throw the dog's tennis ball just as well as righty. Slopped soup on myself the first couple of times, but I got it eventually. Even learned to use a scissors left-handed.

I still do it. I've been ready to have a broken right arm for almost sixty years now. Hasn't happened yet, but if it does, I'm ready.

Peanut Butter Economics This afternoon I spent about ten minutes getting every last bit out of the peanut butter jar. Marie doesn't even throw 'em away anymore when she's done with it, because she knows I'll pull it from the trash, scrape it and get another half a sandwich out of it.

Yeah, I can afford another jar but I grew up watching every penny. It would have hurt my dad and mom if I'd wasted food.

So I didn't. And I don't. I clean my plate, I use the end pieces from the loaf of bread, and I swish a little water in the bottom of the soup can to get the last few bits. Marie doesn't even roll her eyes anymore; it just is what it is.

When my kids or grandkids give me a hard time about cutting the toothpaste tube in half and scraping the insides, or spending so much time and energy with the jelly jar and butter knife, I don't go in to a long story about growing up poor. They've heard it. Now I just tell 'em to fuck off.

Addendum: Granted, economics can't be the only consideration. There was a time when I thought I was having serious intestinal problems.

Turned out to be heartburn. You can't always just scrape the mold off the cheese and eat it. Sometimes you gotta throw the shit away.

Naps   When I'm in bed at night I try to sleep on my side, like I used to. But when I'm on my left side my shoulder hurts, and when I turn over to my right side I can only last about 5 minutes before my hip starts hurting. So I end up waking up a few times and finally resign myself to sleeping on my back.

Things are slowly falling apart. My body was good for a long time and served me well, but like my old T-bird, the miles piled up and it just started wearing out. One part at a time. So the old Ernie machine needs more time in the garage.

My dog Rocky doesn't always make the best decisions -- and next time he unrolls the toilet paper and runs around the house with it I'm taking the **Sunday** paper to his ass -- but about naps he has it right.

Every now and again we both take a "power rest."   Just a quick nap so I don't later fall asleep in my chair with my mouth hanging open; that's an open invitation for the grandkids to play marshmallow basketball.

I already told you about having to pull the old ball sack out from between my legs when I lie on my back. No big deal; if that was the worst thing about aging I'd be smilin'. But these days I need more recovery time than I used to, so I take a cue from Rocky.

Quick power nap, and then stretch. Rocky gets up from his nap and stretches for a full minute, and he's a strong agile dog. This old dog is trying to be the same.

And a long time ago my son Tony gave me a dark blue Everlast hooded sweatshirt for when I do roadwork ('jogging') in the fall. It's great for naps; pull that hood over my head and 'lights out' … the world goes away.

ps … why the hell did the boxing term 'roadwork' go away? I see people out there all the time running along the road, but they're 'jogging'. Looks like work to me.

Outdated   This one doesn't really fall in this section, but it's a thing I do -- for my own amusement -- so, wtf.

I have always liked the reaction on kids' faces when they have no idea what I'm talking about. When I use a phrase that used to make perfect sense, but not anymore. And I'm not talking about 'roll down the car window' or 'look in the ice box' or 'you sound like a broken record'. Yeah, those are outdated and we don't use 'em anymore, but the kids know what the hell we're talking about.

I mean the phrases that make them screw up their faces into *"what?"* Case in point: A long time ago when my son Tony was a young man he was having some girl problems. He really liked this girl and was having trouble figuring out how to ask her out. I gave him a couple of ways, and told him not to worry if one or the other didn't work: *"There's more ways to skin a cat than just sticking his head in a boot jack and pulling on his tail."*

He had no idea what I was talking about, but he left shaking his head and smiling. Then he asked her out, and she said 'yes'.

Twenty or so years later I was helping Tony coach his son Sam's baseball team, and after a pick-off play worked I looked at our team and said that our pitcher *"faked him out of his jock strap!"* I know that not one kid there was wearing, quite possibly had never seen, a jock strap. Their expressions were great.

Later one of Sam's teammates fouled off three pitches that weren't over the plate, and then took a called third strike on one that was right down the middle. I told the kid, *"What are you looking at? That ball was right down the cock*!" Tony: "Da-ad…" Me: "*Sorry*." But I wasn't; I could hear the rest of 'em giggling behind me.

I try not to cuss too much around them, but sometimes they piss me off and I just tell 'em, *"…and the horse you rode in on."* Someday they'll figure it out and I'll have to deny I ever said it. For now they give me that crooked smile and 'o-kay, grandpa, whatever you say'.

Same thing when I catch them in a fib, or an *'almost fib'* as Maggie Marie calls it (she'll grow up to be a lawyer).

Or when they give me a wild-ass reason why they want something and I tell them, *"You're pissing on my boots and tellin' me it's raining. It ain't raining; tell me the truth."*

They might not know what I'm talking about, but they get a mental picture of pee on a boot and tell me the truth.

There's a few others … when the grandkids say to Marie "grandpa is weird" and she replies "yeah, but I'm stuck with him" I grab her around the waist and tell them *"that's because I'm a hunka hunka burning love!"* They don't know Elvis, so it just gets an 'ewww' out of them.

But speaking of burning love, one thing I do every day is tell them that I love them. Starting with Marie, and if the kids are around and even the little prick grandkids, I tell them too. I do love 'em, and I don't want it to be a secret that I take to my grave. What good is that?

When I was growing up, that wasn't done. My dad was a man's man, more stoic than emotional even though he was Italian. It was rarely if ever said in our house. That's just the way it was.

But that was then and this is now and I changed that habit a long time ago. My family never had to wonder if I loved them and was happy with them, and would be there for them no matter what.

I read that it was Abraham Lincoln who said, "*The best thing you can do for your children is to love their mother.*" No problem there. Marie e`l'amore della mia vita.

A Thing I Will Do Eventually … but hopefully not too soon. When I was in college I had a friend named John who went to Indiana University and was in pre-med. I went down to IU one weekend, and while we were in a Bloomington bar playing pool he described, in intricate detail, how he and some other students were working on a cadaver that week.

They were practicing surgery, opening up the head (I guess with a saw) and working on the brain, and while I was lining up a 3-ball bank shot he was describing cleaning out arteries on this dead guy.

I was morbidly fascinated, and I never forgot that conversation. John is a surgeon now, in Minnesota, and he's a very good one. Part of the reason for that may be that he got to practice on a guy who would never complain about it or sue him for malpractice. (If John were to slip with the knife, he got a do-over because ... 'hey, the guy is already dead'.)

So a couple of years ago I saw some information come through the post office that was from a donor organization here in Chicago. They take body donations and send them to all the schools around here---Northwestern, the University of Illinois Medical Center, Rush, and some others. The line "body donor program for medical science" took me back to that bar in Bloomington, and fascinated me all over again.

I thought about it for a while and then I decided, in spite of Marie's hesitation, that I would sign up. When the time comes that I breathe my last breath, I will donate the Ernie machine to the University of Illinois. They can work on any part of it; I won't care, because, like that guy John was working on, I'll be dead.

And when those young doctors-to-be that were leaning over my corpse finally get their license, and are about to see their first patient, that guy won't be dead. So if they are going to have a *"Whoops! Shouldn't have done that"* moment, better that it's on a dead guy like me, rather than a live person like Tony or Beth or Michael.

Some Things I Shouldn't Do Yeah, there are some things I do that maybe I've worn out. Like when Marie pauses after she says 'I've been thinking …' and I jump in with *"Really?!"* or *"Finally!"* It's funny to me but it usually ends with a whap to the back of my head.

Or when I'm trying to turn my car in an intersection and a couple of guys are 'strolling' through the crosswalk and talking on their cellphones. I probably shouldn't roll down the windows and tell the guys *"Come on, girls, move it along."* My daughter used to hide her head when she saw that one coming.

And I have to stop ignoring pains in my body—in my back or my knee or ankle. Sometimes even in my neck. It's an old habit from when I was young and strong.

I don't know what makes me think it'll just go away; 9 times out of 10 it's not just a little aggravation, it's a warning: **"It's going to get worse if you don't take care of it!"** Should come with a flashing red light and a buzzer.

Those are some things I do, and some things I shouldn't do. Should *you* do 'em? Who the hell knows?

Dr. Ernie just gives options; what you do with them is your own damn business. Pay at the door.

Ernie del Santo

Time is Short, Wrap It Up

The older I get the more often random thoughts pop into my head out of nowhere. I'll be walking the dog and a memory from 50 years ago jumps in, as clear as 50-dollar vodka.

Our sixth grade class going to the zoo and throwing food to the polar bears; Marie and our kids posing in front of the Golden Dome at Notre Dame; the look on Michael's face on his first day of school --- so proud of his little self. Beth in her wedding dress. All of us laughing when Tony shook up Uncle Vinnie's beer can before he gave it to him at Christmas. Little moments.

We all went snorkeling in Hawaii one year; I went underwater about ten feet and looked up at my whole family --- swimming, looking at the tropical fish and as happy as I'd ever seen them. I have that snapshot in my head. Best 'too-much' money I ever spent.

These random memories usually bring a small smile to my face; they're part of the history of my life. A guy like Paul Newman could've watched himself on the screen any time he wanted. Part of the history of his life is right there.

For the rest of us, some of the movies of our life are black and white and faded color snapshots, home movies in a box in the garage, and right here --- in my head.

ps ... Paul Newman was one of the guys I looked up to, because he was not just a good actor but he enjoyed his life. He loved his wife, loved his job and gave a boatload of money to charity. And had fun doing it. I still buy his salsa and popcorn. Probably saw Butch Cassidy twenty times. But I digress...back to wrapping it up.

This Life And That Life   There was a woman who shuffled in to the post office every Friday. She was old from the day I met her. Every Friday without fail for over fifteen years, here she comes, mailing a few letters and buying stamps.

Polish woman (what?) who had a lot of grandkids, and she wrote real letters to them all regularly. When it wasn't busy she would talk about them -- spread all over the United States -- and how she missed them. Then one Friday about a year ago it was five o'clock and we realized she hadn't come in this week.

So we called. She passed in her sleep. I had no idea she was 90. Thinking about her moving from this life to that life, whatever that life is, makes me think about my own afterlife. I don't dwell on it, but I think about it. What if all the priests and nuns weren't exactly correct in their assessment of what would happen.

After all, there's a whole lot of priests that got caught doing things that qualify as 'go-straight-to-hell' mortal sins, so who knows? Do I completely buy everything that they and the nuns were selling?

These are the same nuns who would whack us across the hands and tell us we'll learn the right way or that lesson will travel *"through the skin to the brain."*

And as often as they threatened us with going to hell, I never really bought the idea of eternal fire and brimstone. Maybe temporary, but eternal revenge for some sin like skipping Mass and going to the Dog N' Suds to hang out with girls doesn't seem to fit in with the rest of their 'all-loving' teachings.

And I also think, though they tell us the opposite, that if Robin Williams or someone else who was so depressed, arrived in heaven and said to God "I just couldn't take it anymore" God might have thrown his arms around their shoulders and said "I understand."

So I go my own way on that. I sit in church and listen to the good parts and dismiss what doesn't make any sense to me. Mostly I'm in church to be with folks who are trying to be good people. Hanging out with them for an hour (or more; some of these priests have a lot of wind to blow) makes me want to do the same.

Way too often, though, when I'm sitting in Mass listening or contemplating life and the hereafter, and we're in the middle of the sermon, suddenly jabba the hut shows up at the end of the pew and wants everybody to move down.

So instead of looking at the statue of St. Joseph and getting a little inspiration for the week, I'm crowding my ass next to the other people who got here on time, thinking, *"Hey, ya prick, Mass started a half hour ago. Buy a fucking watch."* Not the thoughts I should be thinking in church.

But I don't think I'll go to hell for that. Maybe spend some time in purgatory. Or maybe none of that is what lies on the other side; maybe God thinks reincarnation would be fun for him. I'll find out one day, hopefully not too soon. And hopefully not after Marie. Couldn't imagine being old without her.

I read once that a guy was dying and right before he breathes his last breath he looked at his family and says, *"Well, this should be interesting."* He closed his eyes and never opened them again. I agree; it will be interesting. A long time from now. Hopefully.

Ernie del Santo

Geezers On Facebook   I know it's not what the
Harvard kid had in mind when he started Facebook, but a
lot of us old folks are using it---- and because of that,
chasing away all the young folks.

I used to regret not staying in touch with family that had
moved away, or with college and high school friends that
left the city. We drifted away, developed our own worlds,
and a Christmas card with an annoying 'recap' letter was
about it.

Then this kid Zuckerberg came along, and Facebook beats
email by a mile. I read it once a day now, and the good
thing is I don't have to ask what they're doing. There it
is, just look at it: this high school friend has a grandkid
playing at Purdue, this other guy that I went to high
school with just sold his business and bought a cabin on
Bass Lake, my old girlfriend from high school just
dumped her third husband (whew).

When I was in grade school my cousin Al was a great
friend. Lived three blocks away and we rode bikes
together, played pinball – him on one flipper and me on
the other 'cause we only had one quarter. Best of friends.

Now that he's moved to Boston, I can not only stay in
touch with him, but his information comes with a
complimentary picture of what the knucklehead had for
lunch.

It's overkill, sure, but it's ok with me. I want to know about the people I used to spend time with; they were part of my history too. And now I can keep up. And send them a picture of Maggie Marie looking up at my nose hair.

So I don't begrudge Zuckerberg or the guy who put cameras in cell phones (*yes, I know it could have been a woman, don't interrupt.*) their gazillion dollars. They changed my life a bit.

Bucket List   My bucket list is a lot like other people's – most of it involves traveling. We've saved enough to go somewhere most every year, often at the spur of the moment. I try not to plan too far in advance … I did that once in the late 70's.

Back then we decided that we were going to go to Italy; to Rome, to the Vatican, see the Pope. I had some vacation at the post office saved up, so we were going to splurge, figuring we'd better do it soon before we have too many kids.

Beth was still young enough to fly free if we fudged on her age a bit. Good thing she was a small kid. They weren't going to send me to purgatory for that --- we were going to see the Pope. And just because I didn't exactly buy the whole notion of hell, it's been a life-long goal to see the Holy Father.

So, in '78 we plan the trip. We get the details set, we'll go next fall, and suddenly Pope Paul dies. Ok, they elect a new one a few weeks later, Pope John Paul, (or, as Vinnie called him, Pope John Paul George Ringo) and he looks like a good man. So we are set; we buy the tickets.

Two weeks later *this* Pope dies! He'd only been Pope for a month. Ok, they elect another one and we're good to go. In fact, John Paul II really seemed like a good guy, not an Italian but a Polish guy (what?) and I was figuring out ways to talk my way into the Vatican and meeting him.

"Your Holiness, I'd like you to meet my wife Marie, our son Anthony, and our baby Elizabeth." I saw it so clearly.

So the summer of '79 is coming and we are looking forward to traveling. We notice that this Pope is also a traveler, and he's going to go around the globe and meet his Catholics. And where is he going? In the fall, at the exact time that we will be in Rome? That's right. Grant Park, Chicago.

Marie, Tony, Beth and I were in Rome at the exact same time the Pope was in Chicago saying Mass in Grant Park. We were at his house and he was at ours.

We still had a great time in Italy; went to the Vatican, to my grandparents villa south of Florence, met some relatives. It was great, but I have to think that God was getting me back for cussing so much and eating hot dogs on Friday in the 60's.

Tony   Thinking of little Tony hopping around Italy, chasing birds out of the square and laughing when he saw the anatomically-correct statues reminds me of the time when he was in 8th grade, and the counselor there was asking him about college. Tony wasn't too interested in college, he wasn't even 14 yet, so he had a little fun with them.

Remember when I told that he shook up Vinnie's beer can and laughed like a hyena? That's him. And I used to make them all watch Rocky and Bullwinkle when they were kids --- lots of education in those cartoons --- so when the counselor asked him where he wanted to go to school, he told her "*a smaller school in Minnesota.*" "Oh, what school is that?" With a straight face he told her, "*Wossamatta U. It's in Frostbite Falls.*" "Oh, uh-huh. I think I've heard of that school. Ok."

She wrote it all down and it showed up on their 'Class Ambitions' yearbook page. I can still see that grin on his face, all these years later. Again, I digress ….

Back to the Bucket List   Marie and I both want to go to Tokyo or Beijing or to India. Somewhere completely different from anywhere we've ever been, geographically and culturally. And, like everybody else, I think it would be fun to ride an elephant. Sue me.

One thing I'd like to do, a little closer to home, is something we used to do a long time ago as a family. We rented a small cabin in Michigan for a week in August. We didn't have cell phones and there was no tv reception, so it was just us, nature, and a small radio.

We hiked, we fished, we shined flashlights at raccoons and owls, cooked popcorn over an open fire and took turns ruining songs on the harmonica. Had fishing contests and I made sure that Beth won every one of them. They knew I was cheating but they'd won all the tree climbing and swimming contests, so tough shit.

Just once I'd like to do that with all the kids and grandkids, nephews and nieces. The whole family; unplug and go. I know that they would sneak their phones in but if they didn't watch 'em in front of me I'll be fine with that. That's the top of my bucket list --- the whole family looking each other in the eyes as they have fun together.

Maybe for my 75th birthday they'll humor me, and we'll all go up there for an "Ernie-palooza". Is that a big enough hint, guys?

I am grateful for the fact that my kids have always loved each other. And I think a lot of it had to do with the fact that we made them bunk together, even though we had the room.

Tony and Beth had bunk beds until Beth was 8, and then it was Tony and Michael. I could hear their little voices talking after lights out, and in the morning the first thing they saw was each other. I'm convinced it bonded them.

There's a picture of Tony and Michael putting their arms around Beth at her wedding ... all three of them mugging for the camera; big, proud smiles full of love. A love partly built by those late-night conversations. And by being Marie's kids. That's our legacy, right there.

Sometimes on Facebook I see pictures that a guy took of his kids, one every month for twenty years. I wish I'd thought of that. If I had, it would be that pose—the three of them with their arms around each other's shoulders. I don't really have to see the snapshots though; I got 'em right up here.

Gratitude   A little advice from Dr. Ernie: compliment one of us gray-hairs today. Tell the old fart that he or she looks good and that you're happy to see 'em. Make somebody's day.

You'll see the very definition of gratitude. Be genuine and sincere and you'll see a look on their face that is the epitome of gratitude ... as long as you don't follow it up with "*for your age.*" Remember what I said about that: they might not say 'fuck you' but they'll think it.

Wrap It Up Already   So when I reminisce I guess I
don't have too many complaints. Regrets? I have a few,
like the Chairman Of The Board sang, but too few to
mention.   Still, there are times that I regretted not going
to 'Nam like a lot of my friends. I was a good
typist/analyst and they kept me stateside. But I thought
then and now that it was a senseless war, and some of
those guys didn't come back, like my high school friend
Tim.   So I'm not sure it's officially a regret.

I may have one regret pretty soon … Beth started reading
this book and said, *"Do you have to use my real name?"*
I said, "Don't worry, honey, I'll change all the names."
I lied.

Speaking of Beth, one time when she was about 22 or so
she wanted to learn to play golf. I had heard that a guy
that I used to play baseball with was teaching golf at an
academy up north of O'Hare.   Jeff was a great baseball
player and a great golfer and I knew he could teach her
more in one lesson than most guys could in ten. But I
hadn't seen Jeff in over ten years.

So I called the place where he was working, he comes on
the phone and all I say is "Jeff, who's the best third
baseman you ever played with?" He immediately says *"It
sure as hell wasn't you. A good third baseman would
have made that catch against the Jays in the playoffs."*   If
you had a sports camaraderie once, you still have it.

Back to those random thoughts … I think back to times in my youth when I was a flirty kid, a prankster. I would often tease young girls in school; some of those girls I haven't seen in 50 years but once in a while I still think about them and wonder if they ever think about me.

I remember the time back in 7th grade when I was an altar boy and after Mass had the job of bringing back the water and wine cruets to be dumped out and washed. I took the wine that was left, put it in my mouth, finished my chores and walked home … with the wine still in my mouth.

I went in to Vinnie's room, pointed to my cheeks, swallowed, and breathed on him "aaahhhhhh!" *"You stole the wine!!"* I told him it wasn't stealing, they were gonna throw it out, so no confession needed.

From then on it became a thing; which altar boy could get the most wine in their mouth and hold it the longest. A kid named Frank got caught so that was the end of that.

There was a line in a John Denver song *"turns me on to think … of growing old"* and I'm not sure it turns me on, but it sure is interesting. I don't want to be any younger than I am; *"Hope I die before I get old"* was a good line by the Who, but I'm glad I was around for all the things that happened in my 50's and 60's.

It's a big effort though, to be a cool old guy and not be a crusty old curmudgeon. Still working on it. There are times when I hurt or creak and I think I've got it bad, and then I see this one old guy who only has one arm and he rides his bicycle everywhere. And I think, maybe I don't have it so bad.

But then I can't find my damn reading glasses so I get up from the couch and go to step over the ottoman and the damn thing reaches up, grabs my foot and trips me.

Getting old sucks.

FINE

GLOSSARY

"…and the horse you rode in on."   The second half of a sentence, often used when I'm accompanied by children, elderly ladies, or clergy. The full sentence is: "Fuck you … and the horse you rode in on."

Asshat   A guy who has his head up his ass, thus … wearing his ass as a hat.

Bill Murray   Carl Spackler in Caddyshack. *"'…uh, there won't be any money, but when you die, on your deathbed, you will receive total consciousness.' So I got that goin' for me, which is nice."*

Chuck Wepner   former heavyweight boxer, aka The Bayonne Bleeder. He got cut up a lot, but was a warrior. Went 14 ½ rounds with Muhammad Ali.

Coke plant   In a steel mill, coke (not the kind you snort or drink) is made from coal, taking out the impurities. Hot, dirty place. If you had to work in the steel mill, you wanted to work on the steel side or in the tin mill. You didn't want to work in the coke plant.

Come ti vidi m'innamorai, e tu sorridi perché lo sai.
"When I saw you I fell in love, and you smiled because you knew." Arrigo Boito

GLOSSARY

CRS   the non-clinical term "Can't Remember Shit". In some cases it's really MCI, Mild Cognitive Impairment, a real thing; it doesn't necessarily lead to Alzheimer's or dementia but it's annoying as hell.

Culottes   Women's pants that resemble shorts. <u>Women's</u>. And when women wear them, you usually cannot see their underwear from across the street.

CYO   The Catholic Youth Organization that sponsored a boxing tournament. Sometimes when I got hit hard there it felt like an epiphany.

Dumb As A Hundred Chickens   My Uncle Mac worked on a farm and used to say that. Dumb as a post, dumb as a box of rocks; same thing.   Doesn't mean they're bad people, just not too bright.

FINE Italian.   The End.

Frickin'   The more civil term, used when kids are around; I say "you frickin' idiot" but I really want to say "you fucking asshole."

Gabriela Sabatini   Great women's tennis player; one of the few reasons men watched women's tennis in the late 80's. From Argentina.

GLOSSARY

Heartbreak Hill   Originally known as the steep hill in Boston at about the 20-mile mark of the Boston Marathon. Now it's pretty much any hill in my way.

Illegitimus non carborundum est   Latin. "Don't let the bastards grind you down."

Kool A menthol cigarette old men smoked in the steel mill. I inhaled one once. One of the ten worst tastes my mouth has ever experienced.

Irish Wake   Punch lines from page 51 (which you should already know). *What's the difference between an Irish wake and an Irish wedding? One less drunk at the wake. What happens with either an East Texas divorce or a tornado? Somebody's gonna lose a trailer.*

L'amore della mia vita The love of my life. See? Old crusty guys can be romantic.

Purgatory   A temporary hell, when you've been bad but not that bad. Possibly my next home.

Ralph Kramden   One of the greatest characters in the history of television, played by The Greatest: Jackie Gleason. Ralph was a bus driver with a big heart and a body to match. "To the moon, Alice!" "Norton!"

GLOSSARY

Rap Music   A contradiction of terms. Rap, crap.
Synonyms.

Salute`   Italian. *"Cheers!"* Often said by old men with
wine or cute little girls with milk.

Take-Down   A wrestling move, taking a guy from the
standing position to the mat. It used to take a very tough
guy to get a take-down on me; now a dog toy left on the
kitchen floor can do it.

Tom Harmon's Son   NCIS actor Mark Harmon. Good
actor; used to play football at UCLA.

> *Do not go gentle into that good night,*
> *Old age should burn and rave at close of day;*
> *Rage, rage against the dying of the light.*
>
> *- Dylan Thomas*

About The Author

Interested in learning more about the author, Mr. del Santo? His interests, his hobbies, his family life and upbringing? Just log on to

www.noneofyourfrickinbusiness.crap

Made in the USA
San Bernardino, CA
26 May 2016